everyday flowers

PREVIOUS PAGE A single mini green cymbidium orchid head is arranged in a votive.

THIS PAGE Long French peach tulips in single vases make a simple but effective mantelpiece design.

OVERLEAF LEFT A scented *Narcissus*.

OVERLEAF RIGHT Pompon Santini chrysanthemums are combined with the standard 'Tom Pearce' and arching stems of rose hips.

PAULA PRYKE

with photography by Rachel Whiting

everyday flowers

FLOWERS TO BEAUTIFY AND DECORATE THE HOME

RIZZOLI
NEW YORK

New York · Paris · London · Milan

First published in the United States of America in 2012 by
Rizzoli International Publications, Inc.
300 Park Avenue South
New York, NY 10010
www.rizzoliusa.com

Originally published in the United Kingdom in 2012 by
Jacqui Small LLP
an imprint of Aurum Press Ltd
7 Greenland Street
London NW1 0ND

PUBLISHER Jacqui Small
MANAGING EDITOR Kerenza Swift
EDITOR Sian Parkhouse
ART DIRECTOR Sarah Rock
ILLUSTRATOR Hannah McVicar
PHOTOGRAPHER'S ASSISTANT Corin Ashleigh Brown
PRODUCTION Peter Colley

2012 2013 2014 / 10 9 8 7 6 5 4 3 2 1

ISBN: 978-0-8478-3715-1

Library of Congress Control Number: 2011937537

Printed in Singapore

In loving memory of Coco—my
constant companion for the last
fourteen years, who particularly
enjoyed our days in the garden

contents

introduction

This is my most personal book, as it has been almost
entirely shot in my home and garden. It is not about the
kind of flowers I arrange for clients; it is a book filled
with the simple flower arrangements that I make for
my own pleasure or to share with my family and friends.
Like the cobblers' children who go without shoes, I often
bring flowers home from work but suffer from a lack of
time to arrange them, abandoning them in the simplest
vase to fend for themselves. This is especially true when
entertaining. After you have shopped and prepared your
food, decorating the table is a last-minute, rushed affair.
However, simple, natural arrangements, using store-
bought blooms and flowers or foliages from your garden,
are straightforward to achieve, even under time pressure,
and these are the arrangements that I like the most. I
hope that in this book I have offered some easy ways to
make your home more beautiful and fragrant with
seasonal flowers.

   The message is easy: keep it seasonal, fresh, scented,
and simple. Enjoy!

flower shapes and color

The shapes and colors of flowers are captivating. As children we are often drawn to their simple shapes: dandelions with their spherical seed heads and daisies in a carpet of green are the first to be plucked. As gardeners we can become obsessed with the height and shape of flowers and where we are going to place them to get the best out of the plant. Both approaches are key when selecting flowers for arranging to get the most enjoyment out of a successful arrangement. If I am making a large arrangement, for example, I want to use a mass of flowers and foliages with very different shapes and textures. I will need some tall spire-shaped flowers, such as delphinium, *Eremurus*, or gladioli in summer. In spring I rely on the tall branches of blossom and catkins. For smaller arrangements I am drawn to short stems or miniature flower heads that are more delicate. The right combination of flower shapes is as important as the choice of color. It is all about balance and proportion. A good choice creates a great arrangement that can make your heart miss a beat when you see it.

Umbels or flat-headed plants are among my favorite shapes. I adore the shape of cow parsley, and I use a lot of *Anethum graveolens* in my arrangements because I like the color, smell, and texture. It makes a great filler and plays a supporting role to other flowers.

ABOVE LEFT I am drawn to berries such as this fruiting ivy, for their texture and great architectural shape.

LEFT Flat heads of sedum and *Trachelium* make good fillers in large arrangements and give great cover in textural rings and dense hand-tied bouquets.

OPPOSITE, CLOCKWISE FROM TOP LEFT Some flower shapes, such as bluebells and this 'Minos' hyacinth, have a more complicated habit and structure. They look great when massed on their own, and also

work well mixed with other seasonal spring flowers.

Bold shapes, like these seed heads of the lotus, or *Nelumbo nucifera*, are always useful.

I never tire of the daisy shape; the Japanese anemone, for example, is a happy flower and works well in lots of situations and surroundings.

Tall grasses or this barley, *Triticum aestivum*, lend a more natural or vegetative feel so they often feature in flower arrangements for my home.

containers

Arranging flowers from your garden throughout the seasons requires a good selection of vases. If you start with a badly designed vase or a poor shape, even the most experienced arranger cannot create a good arrangement. You need to have a choice of vases that suit the kind of flowers you want to use and the effect you hope to achieve. It's not a level playing field when it comes to vases, as some designs always produce better results.

Look for the types of vase that I use in this book, and start to create a stock of alternatives for the different seasons. Basic everyday vases in glass ranging from 4 to 8 inches in height for table flowers are a must. I always suggest a range of glass cube vases from 4 to 8 inches, so that you can use one inside the other and adapt them throughout the year. The 6-inch cube is my most-used vase. Bottles are useful for single stems, so a collection that works well together on a mantle or side table is worth looking out for. Save old jam jars to cover with sticky tape and leaves, and terra-cotta pots always look the part for outdoor dining. For taller arrangements, thinner vases 6 to 12 inches wide and 24 inches or taller in height are necessary for branches, tall flowers, and large-headed flowers. Pitchers always work well with mixed bunches, herbs, and grasses, as do decorative watering cans. A group of glass cylinder vases at different heights and widths is always useful.

LEFT I spotted these giant teacups and used them for an Alice in Wonderland children's tea party. The mad mix of spotted color was an invitation to use an array of colors. On a base of dark green ivy berries, mini sunflowers dominate a mix of red nerines, fronds of green dill, and asters. The black seed heads of agapanthus look like mad spiders trying to strike out from the arrangement!

OPPOSITE Japanese lacquer works so well with natural containers and here three simple coconut shells nestle on a gold-leafed platter. One head of 'Teddy Bear' sunflowers in each shell makes a very simple, inexpensive, and effective table center.

raiding your closet

Your kitchen cabinets contain an assortment of items that work very well combined with flowers and foliages. Over the years I have been tempted to use some of these items in my work for restaurants or for creating themes for parties. For a long time I have been using brightly colored candies to make fun containers for children's birthdays, bar mitzvahs, or other celebrations. Wrapped candies can be wired into cones and topiary shapes, too. Pink and white marshmallows look good inside vases with pale flowers, while the more brash color schemes of chocolate-coated beans or jelly beans work for Halloween, Thanksgiving, or the festive season. As well as carving pumpkins, I always make a festive food and flower arrangement with my girls in the fall, and we often make a wreath for the door as well. We use corn, gourds, and capsicums for this, as well as rose hips and berries. There are a wealth of products that are sold on the flower auctions, mostly fruit and vegetables that are too small for the supermakets or are not edible, such as solanums or *Cucumis*. Dried pulses, pasta, and coffee beans can also make interesting effects when added to vases. Swirls of pasta add color and texture. Coffee beans not only look lovely, they smell good, too. Finally, nuts can be interesting for winter arrangements, and cinnamon and star anise are favorites of mine, for their scent and the texture they add to the Christmas festivities.

THIS PAGE A cylinder vase was placed inside a round bowl, and swirls of different pulses were added to the base and then some nuts and dried fruits and beans. Inside the internal container I added a generous bunch of open Iceland poppies. I always make sure the ends have been singed with a naked flame when using poppies, to ensure longevity.

OPPOSITE This arrangement was inspired by the sticky buds that form in the spring on chestnut trees. A long shallow tray was filled with a thin layer of floral foam, and the structure was created with the branches, Clooney ranunculus, and some tubes and swirls of dried pasta. A touch of hebe, some wonderful fatsia berries, and a few rhubarb stems add texture to the arrangement.

This season is one of nature's annual miracles. Spring is a welcome relief after the dormant period of winter. It is the antidote for those of us who are anxious to get back out into the garden and see the renewal of all plant life.

spring

I was raised in East Anglia, in the east of England, and have now returned there to live. This is one of the most important arable farming areas of Britain and it often seems to me that the landscape of winter is in fact mud! If, like me, you love to have a garden of perennials and annuals, you are also surrounded by bare earth as many of the plants have retreated beneath the ground to escape the frosts and cold temperatures of the winter. As they emerge, the first flowering bulbs start to look like they came dressed for a party, and as the days go on, they get stronger, the blooms more plentiful, and they become quite exquisite. Many of the bushes start to show blossom or catkins. The wild hedges have the silky tassels of the hazel family. I am married to an architect, and the plants found in my garden can reflect this. Birches have crept into our landscape—they are loved by architects for their statuesque qualities and their gleaming white bark stems. The two varieties we planted have different catkins, and in spring they take quite different forms before their leaves arrive. I love the spiky textural tassels of witch hazel, and even though this plant does not like the soil conditions in my garden, I keep them and camellias in pots with ericaceous soils and have to feed them to support good buds in spring. Sometimes you can spend a long time nurturing your camellias only to have them all struck by a harsh frost. Occasionally gardening can be disappointing, which I think is what makes the triumphs and the successes so much more gratifying. Failures or damage by natural causes are all part of the cycle. The saying "I may be old but I am still a young gardener" is so true; there is so much to learn each year in the garden.

RIGHT 'Dutch Master': nothing else says spring as definitively as a mass of the classic trumpet *Narcissus* in a true daffodil yellow of ducat gold. These are perfect tall and erect bulb flowers, which work well growing in a natural fashion through fresh green long grass.

THIS PAGE These are the male catkins of the common hazel, *Corylus avellana*. Pale yellow and around 2 inches long, they are usually at their best in February when the lambing season is just about to start. Their common name is lambs' tails, and they look lovely with daffodils in simple vases or pitchers.

OPPOSITE, CLOCKWISE FROM TOP *Primula vulgaris*, or common primroses, are easy to grow and work well in the garden grown alongside varieties of *Narcissus*.

A real beauty of a hellebore, the 'Winter Sunshine' variety is a long-lasting plant in the garden, and it makes a good cut flower, too.

The white-stemmed *Betula utilis* var. *jaquemontii* is a wonderful statuesque tree in winter and has the added bonus of these great catkins in spring, before the leaves start to develop.

what's good
in the garden

When spring returns, walking around your garden can be like arriving at a party and finding that lots of really good friends have turned up. I love looking around the garden greeting the signs of new life. After I have enjoyed the first snowdrops of winter, I wait patiently for the hellebores. One moment they are looking beaten by the weather and then one day, almost by magic, they are showing their flowers.

The early spring bulbs of the *Narcissus* family are very rewarding and ask little of the gardener, returning each year to delight. There are still lots of lovely ivy berries to mix with a few spring flowers at this time of year, and there are also many early flowering shrubs that become the backbone to early spring arrangements. After the pale yellow of the winter jasmine, we have the welcoming bright yellow of the forsythia—excellent for filling tall vases as well as adding short sprigs to a spring collection of garden finds. The pink and yellow of the flowering currant family are very popular. The more common pink *Ribes sanguineum* is a staple of the cottage-style garden. I am also very taken by the creamy yellow *Ribes aureum*, which I planted last year in my new border. The pussy willow and branches of catkins are good for adding texture to tall arrangements, and the glossy leaves of the camellia give good structure. The bergenia family has lovely strong leaves and useful cut flowers. I love the pink varieties, but there are many in this family to choose from, and they are useful ground cover for the first part of the year. Primroses are also reliable, and some varieties of viola are essential to the early spring garden. Even smaller and not so successful as a cut flower are the tiny violas. I prefer to use them planted as decoration and often bring them indoors in pots to make a table center. For scent at this time of year it is essential to plant hyacinths. They return often in future years, but they never seem to have such a great form as the first year they flower, so I try to plant a few each fall to enjoy. My current favorite is the purple 'Woodstock', but I also love the bright pink 'Jan Bos' and 'Delft Blue'.

CLOCKWISE FROM TOP LEFT One of the first plants to flower is the witch hazel. *Hamamelis mollis* is an early harbinger of spring and lasts well in vases as a cut flower.

Bergenia has long been loved by flower arrangers for its lovely strong leaves, but the flowers work well in water, too. A member of the *Saxifragaceae* family, *Bergenia purpurascens* is a newcomer to my garden, and I treasure its early blooms.

The beetroot purple color of the 'Woodstock' hyacinth is one of my current favorite colors to experiment with.

Pussy willow is the common name given to *Salix caprea*, which is a popular spring shrub in many parts of the world. In China it is used to celebrate New Year and in Eastern Europe it is used in Christian Palm Sunday services. It is a plant that has a special place in the hearts and minds of nature lovers all over the world.

This purple cherry with its deeply toned leaves and pale pink flowers is *Prunus x cistena*. It can be grown as a small tree or a bush.

With its scented pink flowers, which appear at the same time as the fresh leaves, *Ribes sanguineum* is a spring garden essential.

OPPOSITE If your budget is limited, spend some time in spring sowing from seed, as this is the cheapest way to get flowering plants established for picking later in the season.

what's good to buy

I always think that spring is such a good time for the amateur flower arranger as the flowers are plentiful, inexpensive, and long lasting. They come in a huge range of colors, and are not too challenging. Perhaps because many of them are quite diminutive, they look lovely very simply arranged in glass vases or pitchers.

The larger flowers work well massed together, and that makes it easier to put a combination together. There are always new varieties of tulips to enjoy, and serrated-edge and double varieties last well and stand rather than droop down, as some tulips do. Branches of blossom and catkins are long lasting if you buy them fresh. Strip the leaves off so the flowers do not compete with the leaves for water. Most commercially grown woody stems are sold with a special flower food, which is best mixed with hot water and then cooled with cold water for better oxygenation.

1 Anemones add jewel colors to the spring palette. Available as a cut flower from November to April, they are happiest in water, not floral foam. This white variety is *Anemone cornonaria* 'Galil Wit'.
2 Few can resist the small pompoms of *Viburnum opulus* 'Roseum' with their tiny green florets. The flowers you buy are greener than the garden shrub.
3 Ranunculus is an enduring favorite flower for me and I love this 'Cappuccino' variety.
4 The huge variety of color and style plus the long season make tulips one of the most versatile and inexpensive of the spring flowers.
5 Veronica is a summer flower for gardeners, but an all-year-round flower for the florist and it works well with delicate spring flowers. Available in pink, blue, and white, it works well with *Muscari*, all types of *Narcissus*, and tulips.
6 Lily of the valley is at its most plentiful and most reasonable to buy in late April or early May, depending on the weather. In France it is traditionally given as a gift for May Day, and it is popular with brides the world over for its delicious scent.

7 Lilac is often sold without the leaf on long straight stems. It can be expensive, but it lasts well, especially if you use flower food. I adore natural lilac cut from the garden because it has the leaf and is usually scented. I like the curvy stems in vases.
8 Reliable and long lasting as a cut flower, the cream scented *Narcissus* 'Avalanche' pictured here and the bright yellow 'Grand Soleil d'Or' are among my favorites and have been an enduring presence in my designs.
9 *Muscari* has a long season and lasts about five to seven days. It is small, so seems quite expensive, but it is a joy in tiny vases and small posies. It is a great choice for spring weddings.
10 Calla lilies are stylish spring flowers. They look good in any environment and are easy to arrange.
11 Blossom is sold from February to April. If you buy the flowers in bud they usually last a week. I like branches arranged on their own in a tall vintage pitcher, or with pink tulips arranged at the base, or with some tall pink lilies.
12 There is something so perfect and appealing about the shape of the camellia flower.

8

9

11

7

6

12

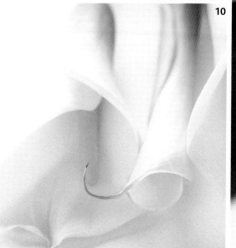

10

growing a cutting garden from seed

Growing flowers from seeds is easy if you have the right weather, and if you sow them at the best time. That is why many people think that you always need a little bit of luck when gardening, as you can never predict what the weather is going to do in the long term.

Reasonably sized seeds such as sunflowers or marigolds will need to be planted 2½ inches from each other. If you are planting poppies then you need to thin them out to give them more space. All this is time consuming, so I limit my seeds to about eight varieties and I concentrate on seeds that I can plant directly where I want them to grow, such as sweet peas into containers, sunflowers in my borders, and marigolds and dill in my vegetable patch. I am spurred on by early successes in the season and sometimes give up too early if the weather is not conducive. The next year one is always up again for the challenge. That is the beauty of gardening.

Among the best annual flowers for cutting are the tobacco plant, including *Nicotiana alata* 'Lime Green' and 'Tinkerbell', which have acid green blooms and *N. sylvestris*, whose stately white flowers look wonderful in a vase. Zinnias are very fashionable and I adore 'Green Envy', although I also love the mixed hot colors. I love the umbrella shapes of *Ammi majus* and *A. visnaga*, which are easy to sow direct into the soil. I also can't get through the year without a clump of *Anethum graveolens*, the green/yellow dill that looks great with most cut flowers and adds a lovely scent. Recently I have

become very taken by *Briza maxima*, the greater quaking grass, which makes lovely informal bunches. *Calendula officinalis* adds some hot color to my herb patch and is so useful for brightening up canapé trays for parties. Cosmos has striking flowers—try 'Purity' for its white blooms and 'Dazzler' for its shocking pink tone. Don't forget stocks for scent either.

Biennials are sown between May and July and will flower the next year, though the trend for instant gratification means that biennals are not as popular. Sweet Willams are good cut-and-come-again flowers. In my garden I cannot resist foxgloves and forget-me-nots, although they can take over. Perhaps the best biennials for cutting are wallflowers—there are many different varieties in different shades. *Erysimum cheiri* 'Fire King', has orange flowers and 'Blood Red' very dark red blooms.

OPPOSITE Cornflowers, sunflowers, larkspur, sweet peas, *Nigella*, and scabious are all easy to grow from seed.

THIS PAGE Hardy annuals are among the easiest you can grow. Sow seed directly into the soil, or in seed trays between March and May, and you will quickly have a supply of flowers.

spring border

For the spring planting scheme we asked Roger Harvey, who is something of a snow drop specialist, but knows as much if not more about hellebores, and has a specialty nursery producing woodland and shade plants in Suffolk, England.

Roger included two backbones to many of my spring designs, the contorted hazel *Corylus avelleana* 'Contorta' and the silver catkins of the violet willow *Salix daphnoides*. He knows I adore a little scent, and the shrubby honeysuckle *Lonicera fragrantissima* is one of the best scents for the spring garden. The handsome *Viburnum* x *burkwoodii* is lovely for small arrangements, and the leaves of the *Brunnera* 'Jack Frost' have beautiful markings. Hellebores and dicentra work well together with a touch of flowering currant. No spring planting plan for me would be complete without a touch of ranunculus, and 'Flore Pleno' produces adorable small round flowers.

1 *Lonicera fragrantissima*
2 *Viburnum* x *burkwoodii*
3 *Corylus avellana* 'Contorta'
4 *Salix daphnoides*
5 *Ribes* 'King Edward VII'
6 *Osmanthus* x *burkwoodii*
7 *Bergenia* 'Overture'

8 *Pulmonaria* 'Opal'
9 *Brunnera* 'Jack Frost'
10 *Synthyris stellata*
11 *Helleborus* x *hybridus* Bradfield hybrids
12 *Helleborus* x *ericsmithii* 'Winter Moonbeam'
13 *Heuchera* 'Obsidian'

14 *Dicentra* 'King of Hearts'
15 *Anemone apennina*
16 *Euphorbia amygdaloides* 'Purpurea'
17 *Ranunculus aconitifolius* 'Flore Pleno'

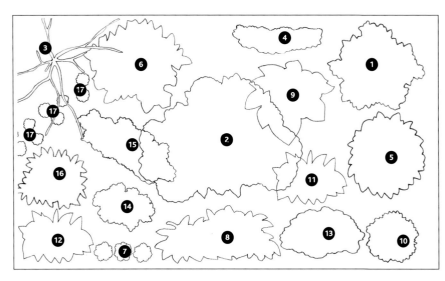

early spring

By the end of February the air starts to smell different, and we feel a yearning to get back out into the garden. For those of us who like to garden, it is now that we start to plan our future planting and we buy seeds to propagate in glasshouses and indoors on windowsills.

By the time the early *Prunus* comes out in the hedgerows and the pussy willow starts to turn from gray to yellow, the days are getting longer and the triumph of spring over the harshness of winter is underway.

Color in the garden comes from flowering bushes, such as the bright yellow forsythia. Later the Japanese kerria produces an abundance of round flowers. Spring is a time for swathes of bulbs, first the *Narcissus* and patches of crocuses, and then the early flowering tulip varieties. In the flower beds the hellebores, the violas, and the primroses look wonderful with the spring snowflakes. The early flowering white snowflakes, *Leucojum vernum*,

are also a great cut flower. They last well, have the appearance of the dainty snowdrop, but are taller and stronger. The countryside can be a mass of white blossom at this time, mostly from the wild blackthorn before the leaves burst open. I adore wild celandine flowers, which are named after the swallow. At one time maybe they flowered at the same time as the swallows arrived. These delicate flowers are a joy to behold on spring walks with wild violets.

It is a great time to enjoy the bud formations on trees, and even use magnolia or chestnut in bud as part of a design. Cutting buds from your fruit trees and enjoying the early advancement of the leaf brings the garden indoors and heightens the anticipation of spring.

The color palette for early spring is mainly pale and delicate, with pink, blues, and whites predominating. Many of the flowers in this period are small and look great together. The other focus color in the garden is yellow, mostly from forsythia and

ABOVE This pretty variety of *Leucojum vernum* is sometimes called the spring snowflake. It flowers from February to March.

daffodils. The highlight is the intense green of the new growth. If you take a walk in the sunshine you can enjoy the luminosity of each blade of grass and each leaf bud as it uncurls.

OPPOSITE There are fifty or so varieties of *Muscari* available as a cut flower on the Dutch auction, far more than you are ever likely to find in a spring bulb catalog! Here the green-blue variety is 'Saffier'. 'Artist' and 'Cupido' are blue varieties, and a good white variety is 'White Magic', shown here interspersed with bunches of *Helleborus niger*.

LEFT The small blue flowers of forget-me-nots are not long lasting when cut, but they are very special in the hearts and minds of many people.

valentine's day

At this time of year there is a huge variety of really inexpensive and beautiful spring flowers. Significant in my affections are ranunculus—for me this is the spring flower of choice for the romantic season. But if you want a flower that has exotic associations, you really cannot go wrong with orchids. Cymbidium, phalaenopsis, or even vanda are all tremendous value as they last for weeks. Keep them out of drafts, away from air-conditioning or heaters, and they can be very rewarding. If these orchids are too expensive their cheaper cousins, known as the Singapore orchids, are almost as long lasting.

LEFT Phalaenopsis orchids are a classic flower. The white looks good in any surroundings and for Valentine's Day I love the pink, purple, and these bicolor varieties. This newer variety is very aptly called Baldan's Kaleidoscope. Single heads are so stunning that they can be laid on a folded napkin.

RIGHT The peachy pink tones look great in hot pink vases. I love experimenting with peach and hot pink used together—as a color combination it is so feminine.

selecting spring whites

cake design

This is simple to make and ideal for birthdays and anniversaries. It can be adapted to any season, and works well in a single color. The design needs a careful choice of plant material if it is to succeed. In this case it looks good enough to eat!

1

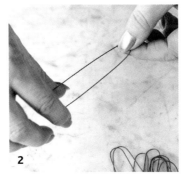

2

3

You will need

- a glass cake stand
- a block of floral foam
- 2 bunches of trailing ivy
- a bunch of *Viburnum tinus*
- a bunch of white hellebores
- a bunch of cream lilac
- a bunch of white ranunculus ·
- a bunch of white anemones
- a sharp knife
- a reel of floral foam tape
- 30 heavy stub wires
- scissors
- a box of thin taper candles

1 Assemble your materials. Cut the foam to fit your glass cake stand. Either use one large foam block or fit several together, securing with floral foam tape.

2 Take a stub wire and bend in half. Continue until you have around 30 hair pins.

3 Use your bent stub wires to pin in the trails of ivy around the sides of the foam block.

4 Continue round the foam so that it looks like the ivy is clinging to the foam and the foam is concealed. Place the foam in the cake stand.

4

5 Next, add the foliage to the top. I begin with the *Viburnum tinus*, creating a full, rounded shape, and then added the hellebores and the woody stems of the cream lilac interspersed among the foliage.

6 Finally, add the taper candles, pushing them firmly into the foam, and the more delicate ranunculus and anemones to finish.

5

6

"The current fashion is for small vases, very simply arranged, and quite random and eclectic. This is a look that works well in the spring, when you can select from a wide variety of flowers and foliages."

OPPOSITE I often find myself in fishing equipment shops, purchasing invisible wires that can take a reasonable weight. The air plants are light and last well without water.

RIGHT Lily of the valley and pussy willow contrast with the star-shaped gray air plant *Tillandsia xerographica.*

BELOW This later flowering single tulip is 'Maureen', and it lasts tremendously well. I love the way they start as the most perfect green and then end up being a warm white color. For me the combination with the alder catkins is sublime.

BELOW RIGHT As a cut flower hellebores can be expensive to buy, so it is best to get a little collection going in your garden.

hanging garden This is a tactile mix of spring flowers and foliages with metal lanterns and hanging *Tillandsia* air plants. From childhood I have always marveled at the excitement of growing bulbs in water, and the roots add interest to the design. I am drawn back to this each year and now do it with my own children. A lot of tulip bulbs that are produced for cut flowers are not grown in soil but by hydroculture. The plant is grown in a special aggregate that absorbs water containing all the nutrients that the plant needs. One of the main advantages is that the growing medium never needs to be replaced. All plants seem to grow very well with this method. It is currently a very popular way to grow plants—particularly spring bulbs—in the flower industry.

easter

Easter for me is a time for more whimsical planted arrangements. The festival of Easter has a long association with flowers, and there is an abundance of inexpensive flowers and small flowering plants available that you can bring together to decorate your home.

For some, Easter means chocolate and the symbolic egg, while bunnies or hares are associated with the holiday as a symbol of new beginnings and fertility. Easter has always been a time to buy flowers and decorate your home for the festival. Many shops do a special window display, and I have even seen some with an egg incubator and real chicks! Over time, this holiday has become more commercial, and now it is common to see boxes of eggs of all sizes at the flower auctions. You can buy huge emu and ostrich eggs, duck eggs, or miniature quail eggs. Of course these are all empty, but if you find the idea of using real eggs not to your taste, there is also a huge range of artificial eggs. With the sap beginning to rise, it is also the best time to use twigs, as a base for an arrangement or a wreath.

LEFT I usually make a large vase of twigs and decorate them with blown and artificial eggs. There are many different species of *Betula*, and the catkins differ. This is *Betula utilis* var. *jacquemontii*.

ABOVE It is a great time for primroses so I often use them in planted baskets lined with sphagnum moss.

OPPOSITE I like egg-shaped vases—it is a pleasing form—and here I have filled the ceramic eggs with ranunculus and stems of green hellebores.

"Pale pink and yellow is an innocent color combination. It suits christenings, birthdays, family celebrations, and carnivals. It is not for the corporate world or romantics."

THIS PAGE A craze that began in Japan for decorative masking or insulating tape gave me the idea for creating a pretty grid for a long low glass vase. The tape is also functional; it holds the ranunculus, *Muscari*, *Viburnum opulus*, and multi-headed *Narcissus* 'Soleil d'Or' in place. Electrical masking tape is usually made in primary colors and can be used inexpensively in the same way with a selection of boldly colored tulips.

easter colors Each season comes with its own unique palette, and the combination shown here has the quintessential Easter colors. Pastels and midrange colors are so readily available in spring. From Easter to the end of May is the best time for cut flowers in my opinion, and there are so many options of color combinations that you can use. Tulips come in a complete spectrum of colors, the range of hyacinths is good, too, and of course I just adore ranunculus. Easter is one of the few times when I might arrange pale pink with yellow. When there is some lime green and china blue, this combination looks very pretty and charming. Speckled miniature quail eggs are nestled among the flowers.

THIS PAGE Miniature arrangements with just five flowers are so sweet; this is a lovely touch on a place setting. You can use votives, or here I used shot glasses covered again with the pretty decorative tape.

late spring

Spring is a season that comes on in a gradual, imperceptible way. One day you open the front door and you can smell that spring is really here. It is the earthy green fragrance of later spring. By this time, it feels like the whole landscape has been given a magic lift.

April is the month of hope and resurgence of life in the landscape. For me late spring is here when I can take my dogs up into the woods and sit in a carpet of blue. I am lucky enough to live very close to some ancient English bluebell woods, and when they come into full bloom I can think of no other place I would rather be on a sunny spring morning.

The majesty of oak and beech trees with swathes of fragrant bluebells is both magical and humbling. It is a reminder to the flower arranger how arresting the use of a single color can be. It is also a lesson in the beauty of simplicity. Currently naturalizing bulbs, or prairie-style gardening, has become very popular.

For me, another spring beauty is the bright yellow celandine. These lovely yellow flowers are very delicate and pretty, and once introduced to your garden they colonize and can take over. The late English gardener Christopher Lloyd found some lesser celandines in a wood near his home and grew them in his famous garden at Great Dixter. These beauties of the ranunculus family are called 'Brazen Hussy', an apt name for a showy little flower. It is certainly a harbinger of warmer climes and was eulogized by the English poet William Wordsworth. This is also the time for dandelions, cowslips, and marsh marigolds, or kingcups as Wordsworth called them, and all remind me of my childhood.

In my garden there is the urgency to get back out and make this year better than last year. April is the month when you want to start cleaning up after the winter. I begin to tidy and start planning new areas of the garden to improve. I enjoy the blossom of forsythia and kerria and the last of the flowering currant. The summer snowflake *Leucojum aestivum* and *Muscari* look good in my beds and make wonderful cut flowers together. Wood anemones push through the earth. Suddenly the very delicate lily of the valley appears as if by magic, and you know that summer is just around the corner. After months of being constrained by length, the blossom and the breaking leaves make the opportunity for large arrangements more achievable.

It is now that the tulips look their best. I have taken to planting tulips in containers as that allows me more

ABOVE A stem of lily of the valley is beautiful to behold and study. The little bells remind me of the flower fairy art by Cicely Mary Barker.

control, and I can move them around the garden to accentuate areas. Most tulips are better lifted and replanted each year and pots make this easier. Once, on a trip to a local nursery, I noticed that they had used lots of old wooden crates as planters, an idea I loved. Over the years I have amassed a shed full of these disused boxes, and now I use them first with spring bulbs and then later in the year with annuals such as sweet peas.

THIS PAGE This test tube ring is one of my favorites for arranging flowers from my garden, as it lends itself perfectly to having twenty-five stems of different varieties and making them into a ring of flowers. It also works well with one flower, or small flowers such as primrose or *Muscari* heads.

"There is something so delicate and magical about the dainty flowers of lily of the valley. They are so romantic and often the first choice for bridal bouquets. I had a few stems wired into my own bridal bouquet and hold this flower very dear to my heart."

keeping it simple Certain flowers are overshadowed or lost if you mix them
with other blooms and are best arranged simply. Snowflakes are native to Europe, they have
straplike green leaves, and the flowers are bell shaped. The spring snowflake *Leucojum vernum*
tends to flower just after the snowdrops in mid-February to March. It establishes
well in cool dampish places in the garden. The summer snowflake *L. aestivum* flowers later
and is an elegant spring cut flower. If you are planning to plant some in your garden,
I recommend 'Gravetye Giant', which is an improved selection with large pure white flowers
tipped in a yellowish green edging. It looks like it has been painted by a fairy but
is a robust variety that can reach 5 inches in height. The stunning beauty has won the RHS
award for merit, and I recommend it to you for exquisite flower displays.

LEFT I love to use bulbs in
spring flower arrangements,
and here we added some
tulips bulbs to the base of
the arrangement and then
added some shallot onions
too! Heads of *Narcissus*
'Minnow' were placed at
the base—creamy white
perianths contrast nicely
with the yellow trumpets.
The round balls of seeds
are from fatsia plants.

OPPOSITE So often in
the spring garden, one is
reminded of the simplicity
of one type of flower in a
vase. Here a few branches
of early pear blossom are
such an interesting color and
shape, they need no
accompaniment.

"So many wonderful things are happening in the garden at this time of year. Everything seems to be bursting forward into lushness."

exploring flower shape

wax bowls

These pretty bowls were inspired by the full, round shape of my favorite spring flower, ranunculus. This is a good activity to try at home with children, but it is a little dangerous, as it involves molten wax and heat. Despite this warning the end results are fun—they make a unique and eye-catching display.

1

2

3

4

You will need
- a double boiler pan
- some colored wax candle-making chips
- a few balloons
- parchment paper
- 50 stems of *Ranunculus* 'Cappuccino'
- lime green skeletonized leaves
- a few stems of pink *Prunus*
- 20 light florist wires
- a roll of gutta percha tape

1 Fill some balloons with water and then tie. Fill the lower pan with water and heat. Add the wax chips to the top of the double boiler. When the wax has melted dangle the balloon into it until it has a good covering. Remove the balloon, wait for the wax to dry a little, and then place on parchment paper. Allow it to dry and set naturally and continue with the next vase. Make 5 or 7, ensuring the wax covers each balloon deep enough to hold water and flowers.

2 When the bowls are dry, lift out the water-filled balloons and you will have some gorgeous vases. Fill with water carefully and then add the individual heads and buds of ranunculus, cut down low.

3 Double leg mount 2 skeletonized leaves together. Continue until you have about 20 sets.

4 Tape over the leg of wire with the gutta percha tape. Continue adding leaves until you have a green garland. Place across the table like leaves around a flower, intertwined with the *Prunus*.

tulip time

Tulips are among the most versatile of all the spring bulbs. They are so easy to grow and thrive in any position where you can give them reasonable drainage. If you cannot find room for them in your borders, grow them in pots; then you can move them around in a kind of grand cross between flower arranging and gardening. The range of tulips available is enormous. I love traveling to the Netherlands for the large fall show as you can buy an astounding variety of tulip bulbs from the airport shops. You can plant tulips any time between October and December, and if you choose a good range of varieties you should be able to enjoy tulips in your garden from February to May. They are easy to grow and very rewarding. I adore the doubles, such as the pale pink 'Angélique', the deep pink 'Queen of Marvel', and the purple 'Blue Diamond'. The double pink one used here is 'Queensland', with the dusty rose color merging to a blush pink. The other variety is 'Huis ten Bosch', which has blossom pink edges merging to white with a deeper rose in the center of the petal. The serrated edge or 'fringed' tulips are a favorite for flower arranging as they are of stunning artistic beauty on their own. The crystalline edges make them look like some spun sugar candy!

ABOVE I enjoy this *Prunus cerasifera* 'Nigra' in my garden because it has delicate pale pink blossom in spring and then lovely purple leaves. This form of the cherry plum is often planted on sidewalks. The pale pink flowers fade to white before the blossom falls and the leaves appear.

RIGHT The combination of blossom and serrated-edge tulips is as close as you get to origami in the flower world. It looks as though someone has cut these out of fine tissue paper; they are so delicate and perfect.

THIS PAGE At home it is hard to beat a good pitcher for a casual flower arrangement. Look for these when you are shopping in kitchen stores or vintage markets. This container suits lots of garden flowers so a variety of sizes is a must.

THIS PAGE The spray rose Olesya ('Intergardia') is given a fragrant touch with early sweet peas and jasmine. A sharp touch of lime green in the form of *Viburnum opulus* and *Thlaspi* lightens the arrangement, and the tiny spires of *Veronica* 'Caya' give movement.

essential filler A new green on the florist's shopping list is *Thlaspi* 'Green Bell'. It is a common 'penny cress' and resembles a weed also known as 'shepherd's purse' because the shape of the fruits were seen to resemble a penny. In France it is called 'monnoyère' from the French word for money and in Germany it is called 'pennywort' after the copper coin Pfennig, which was worth one hundredth of a mark before Germany joined the euro currency. Modern farming pesticides have tried to exterminate this pretty weed on agricultural land, but to no avail. It is fascinating to me that it is now being cultivated, mainly in Israel, as a new wild lime green florist filler from spring to fall. In the same way that it had avoided extermination at the hands of the farmer, its frail stems are amazingly strong and long lasting in the hands of the flower arranger. Here, with a few trails of jasmine, it makes a delicious combination for a special occasion in spring.

THIS PAGE Despite trends and fashions, natural containers always work well with flowers. Here, a bark basket makes the perfect low container for a round tea table arrangement. Always make sure that the flowers tumble over the edge by arranging chicken wire or foam above the edge of the container so you can place some flowers as horizontally as possible around the sides to give a natural effect.

THIS PAGE This collection of late spring beauties—pink bergenia flowers mixed with a selection of hellebores—is arranged in a loose natural way. This kind of simple "just picked" look is romantic and very much the current vogue for weddings.

OPPOSITE White ceramic china looks good with mixed flowers. It is very fashionable to have collections of vases together, with small arrangements or even single stems in each. This makes the maximum impact out of the fewest flowers. Sprigs of flowering currant, forsythia, viburnum blossom, primroses, hellebores, and dicentra sit in tiny irregular-shaped vases.

garden favorites Natural and seasonal flowers arranged simply are such a joy. These pages show two of my loves of the spring garden. Hellebores have become a bit of an addiction, and I constantly collect new varieties. And dicentra, known as 'bleeding heart' by some, is one of my cottage garden favorites. *Lamprocapnos spectabilis* was formerly known as *Dicentra spectabilis*, and it is a wonderful perennial plant that does well in the shade garden. It is very ornamental and for this reason it makes a beautiful cut flower. I adore the pink, but also love the white variety known as 'Alba'. They are animal resistant so in my garden, where I have been plagued by rabbits, they are a must. This enchanting spring flower has retained the "spectabilis." This is Greek for "spectacular" or "worthy of notice"—and here, arranged with other spring beauties, it takes the central stage.

THIS PAGE I adore *Salix* x *sepulcaris* var. *chrysocoma*, more commonly known as the weeping willow. Its arched habit doesn't make it very useful to the flower arranger, but I love to use this tree when the leaves first appear and are not too dense. It makes lovely trailing foliage on pedestal arrangements, and it is pliable enough to be wound around baskets.

celebrating late spring

mother's day

Deep blue and yellow are a lovely combination. Bulb flowers have thick stems and respond better to being in water than floral foam. This basket with a metal liner is perfect for a natural arrangement. Willow is both a symbol of remembrance and fertility, so it is a perfect choice for mother's day!

3 Place the *Brachyglottis* into the bowl first to give the arrangement structure and texture. Add the fleshy stems of hyacinth into the arrangement, making sure that they are placed at different heights, all radiating from one central point. Fill with the rest of the flowers, using the *Muscari* and *Narcissus* in groups for impact.

You will need

- a basket with a zinc liner
- some 2-inch chicken wire
- 15 stems of weeping willow
- 10 stems of *Brachyglottis* 'Sunshine'
- a bunch of blue hyacinths
- 20 stems of *Muscari*
- 2 bunches of *Narcissus* 'Grand Soleil d'Or'
- 10 stems of blue veronica
- 5 stems of purple lilac
- 7 stems of yellow spray rose
- floristry scissors

1 Fill the zinc liner bowl with scrunched up chicken wire so that it is tight and firm. Make sure that the wire comes above the edge of the container so you can get a good rounded shape. Fill with water mixed with flower food.

2 Place the cut ends of the willow in the water through the wire, then weave them through the willow basket.

OPPOSITE This vibrant and scented basket is a perfect gift for your mother to take home after lunch. Keep the zinc bowl topped up and add more flower food to the water to give the arrangement extra longevity. The arched stems of the willow follow the pattern of the basket and make this arrangement appear as a living sculpture. It looks like a vine used this way. The best arrangements are always the ones that mimic nature and look as natural as possible.

THIS PAGE To add a personal touch to the table, place a little bouquet of spring flowers on each napkin. Here they are tied with a stem of willow. *Narcissus* 'Grand Soleil d'Or', *Muscari*, and a few select hellebore flower heads complete this miniposy.

The summer begins for me when I can smell the hawthorn bush and when its white fluffy foliages start to line country lanes. It has a distinctive, sweet musky smell, and it reminds me of walking to school for the summer term.

summer

I have such fond recollections of the hawthorn that I have planted a pink one in my own garden. The countryside is awash with umbels of Queen Anne's lace, and the birds are at their noisiest, building homes or flitting about trying to find food for their newborn chicks. The bluebells in the woods are fading, but in their place one of my top ten flowers is springing up, the breathtaking *Digitalis purpurea*, or foxgloves. As these are biennials they only flower every other year, so in my own garden I keep planting them to ensure I get to see them flowering every summer. I have lots of the purple variety, but I have also sown white f. *albiflora* plants this year. I love the shape of this flower with its elegant bells. Interestingly, it has a long flowering time and I never cut this flower to bring inside, unless one of my chocolate labradors or a strong wind blows them over. Then I will cut them to save their life and place them in a simple bottle in the house. In the summer, the garden gets full and frothy again as all the plants come into their full bloom. The last burst of growth is so sudden and so imperceptible that suddenly you go out one early morning and everything is growing well and in full swing. Everyone is there and they all look their best. There is a euphoric feeling for the gardener as you go around your garden checking off all those flowers you have missed and welcoming them back as old friends. When I see my poppies turn from plump hairy green buds to reveal crumpled papery petals in all their splendor, I know it's powerhose time! Time to clean off the moss and winter's grime and to freshen my garden seating, in preparation for some outdoor entertaining and meals alfresco.

RIGHT Roses are now available all year round, thanks to modern breeding and transportation methods, but nothing beats seeing a beautiful summer-flowering garden rose, such as this yellow David Austin Charlotte ('Auspoly') rose.

what's good in the garden

Summer is truly underway when I stand at my doorstep and can smell the sweet perfume of philadelphus and the musky scent of honeysuckle. If I could bottle that scent I would have to call it the essence of summer. This year I also planted a lot of stock and the freshness of their smell in the evening air is beautiful.

At the beginning of the summer season in my garden, the alliums and the flag irises vie for my attention. They are like siblings shouting "Look at me!" These majestic beauties, which I have mostly in shades of purple, are the stars of the show. Underneath them I still have some scillas, late tulips, and the final flowers on my sweetly scented wallflowers. The foxgloves look wonderful— purple and white spires pop up every other year to my delight. The greens are springing out of the earth and bushes are all starting to take shape. My fig trees are the last to burst forth and one of the last to lose their leaves in the fall. The euphorbia looks splendid, and the hostas and the solomon's seal are early foliage beauties that always attract fans. The overwintered sweet pea seedlings are now racing up to the sun on stakes and begin to produce handfuls of cut flowers that will fill small vases. The peonies look their best in the early summer, and they fade far too fast. Most of my roses begin to bloom in early June and commence their summer performance.

LEFT An old apple tree makes the perfect place for a circular bench to enjoy early summer sun. Summer is full of flowers zooming out of the ground from nowhere, such as these alliums. I grow 'Purple Sensation' and the taller, more spectacular 'Globemaster', which flower from May through to June and sometimes even into July.

ABOVE, CLOCKWISE FROM TOP LEFT
Sanguisorba officinalis is an elegant flower in the garden and popular with bees and butterflies. In flower arrangements it makes a great filler, and it gives movement to vases.

Brown sunflowers such as 'Chianti' or the bicolor 'Ring of Fire' are available to buy in limited amounts, so it's good to grow some.

The foxglove is such a wonderful garden flower that I rarely cut it. It lasts well in a vase, but I tend to leave them where they pop up. Butterflies and bees adore them as well.

Bluebells produce hardy long-lasting cut flowers and will colonize in the right environment.

Echinops are long-lasting flowers in the border and also in the vase. Their shape and texture make them a great addition to any arrangement.

RIGHT Thirsty as a cut flower, sunflowers should be stripped of most of their foliage to help make the flowers last.

FAR RIGHT Solomon's seal, or *Polygonatum*, is at its best in early summer when its green is the most beautiful shade.

OPPOSITE, CLOCKWISE FROM TOP LEFT
Euphorbia characias is a useful perennial. The acid green of these plants looks good from March, but it is at its tallest and most beautiful in June. It forms an excellent backdrop in the garden and offers great foliage in arrangements.

I adore the rich colors of dahlias and their diverse, pleasing shapes. This faithful garden plant produces lots of blooms for cutting.

I love Queen Anne's lace and have included a wild flower section in my garden so that I can enjoy the frilly white waving stems of this most magical of weeds.

Echinacea is such a lovely plant and has a long season. It starts to flower in the summer and goes on to the fall. I have several varieties of coneflower and use it a lot in arrangements.

Don't forget clematis when you think about displaying flowers. These super, versatile climbing plants make surprisingly good cut flowers.

One of the plants that I revere is *Astrantia major.* I have several different varieties in my garden. It is at its peak in June although it flowers for much longer. Here 'Gill Richardson' is doing rather better than some of other varieties I have planted.

RIGHT When I am harvesting flowers from the garden and looking for blooms, I usually take a bucket of water with me. I try to go first thing in the morning or at night when it is cooler.

what's good to buy

Between May and August there is a huge range of flowers to select from at markets and also from retail and wholesale companies. Now is the time to make the most of cottage garden flowers, so look for dianthus in many forms, as well as scented stocks and fragrant sweet peas in an array of wonderful colors.

Mixed colored stocks, or *Matthiola*, are available all year, but they are at their best now and their scent is divine.

The thistle-like flowers of *Eryngium* or echinops make long-lasting flowers if the weather is too hot for more delicate blooms. Now is the time to buy flowering herbs such as mint, *Nigella Origanum*, bergamot, and *Oenothera*, the wonderfully scented evening primrose. Taller flowering plants such as delphinium and larkspur come into their own, as do peonies in all their colors. This is also the prime time for lilies; although they are available all year round they can be bought now for the best value and will be at their longest and strongest.

ABOVE LEFT This old-fashioned sweet William is *Dianthus barbatus*, a glorious deep red. This stem is not fully in flower—when it is the flat head will be a mass of red blossom.

LEFT One historic cottage garden staple is the multi-colored, small-headed, aquilegia, or columbine.

RIGHT *Ammi majus* and *A. visnaga* are the commercial equivalents of Queen Anne's lace, although they both last much better. *A. visnaga* is shown here, with its perfect heads of little florets making up the delicate umbel.

Sweet peas are glorious when mixed together en masse in all their colors. Commercial varieties have larger heads and last better than garden-grown ones.

1 Phlox is a wonderful summer flower. This dainty lady is 'Miss Fiona'.

2 Blue hydrangea is a must during the summer season. The commercially grown flower heads are post-harvest treated and can last really well.

3 Not a very long-lasting flower, campanula does not always travel well as it has masses of little bells down a long stem. However, when you are able to buy it in good condition, it is a stunning beauty. 'Champion White' is a good cut flower.

4 Red peonies are always a favorite, but the season is all too short. 'Scarlet O'Hara' and 'Red Charm' are two of my favorites.

5 *Eryngium* is becoming an all-year-round flower with 'Sirius,' pictured here, being one of the most popular varieties. It has a good color and adds great texture to designs.

6 Zinnias are wonderful summer flowers. I adore the green 'Envy' and the mix of brighter colors. This is the delicate pink zinnia 'Lilliput Rose'.

7 Monarda is a wonderful scented flower with an unusual texture. Its spiky heads give a wild look to arrangements.

8 *Scabiosa caucasica* is never inexpensive to buy, but it is invaluable for summer entertaining, christenings, and weddings.

cutting and conditioning

The best time to cut your flowers is in the morning before the sun hits them, and you need to give them a long drink in a clean bucket with some flower food mixed into the water.

Recut the stems and leave the flowers in a cool place for a while to condition in tepid water mixed with flower food before arranging them. The stem will have sealed over on any flower that has been out of water for a short time, so make a new cut, $1/4$ inch from the end to allow the water to move up the stem, revitalizing the flower and reaching that all-important flower head. The most important thing is that the vase or container you plan to use is as clean as it can be; use household bleach to get rid of any germs. We also use sterilizing tablets for our contract flowers, the type you can buy in tablet or liquid form to clean babies' milk bottles. We have found that these tablets keep the water cleaner, especially if you are using leaves in the vase.

LEFT Cutting stems of *Verbena bonariensis* for summer display: start early in the morning or wait until late at night when the sun is less intense. Make a diagonal cut and place straight into a bucket of water mixed with flower food. Ideally leave in the bucket for a few hours before arranging, as that allows the stem to refresh.

supporting flowers

Any keen gardener will tell you that if you want to grow a lot of tall flowers, such as dahlias, sunflowers, and delphiniums, you need good supports. I own a lot of metal ones that I have collected over the years, which I position in my borders ready for the summer.

Staking and tying is one of the most essential early summer jobs if you want a good border. I like my borders to be stuffed with flowers, like my arrangements. My idea is that if the flowers are all in tight enough they will keep each other up. However, even I have to intervene sometimes. One tip if you don't want to do too much staking is to try to select flower varieties that are closest to the species. The fancier the hybrid the more likely you are to need stakes, as the flower heads can be too weak for the stems. Peasticks are attractive and can be fairly unobtrusive, but sometimes you need the thickness and strength of bamboo.

LEFT I grow my sweet peas and other climbers on topiary frames or wigwams made from bamboo canes. Tying in must be done at regular intervals through the summer, otherwise stems can form a tangled mess. Clematis is especially tricky to disentangle without damaging the stems.

summer border

For the summer planting scheme I approached one of my favorite nurseries and the one I visit at least once a year. Michael Loftus, of Woottens of Wenhaston, is a unique nurseryman with a great reputation and huge range of plants.

This summer border is crammed full with many of my favorite flowers. It makes a wonderful sight and is a great cutting garden if you can bare to snip. This is my favorite color scheme of blues and pink, with a touch of lime green and burgundy. The beautiful blue daisies of catananche would look lovely arranged with the burgundy astrantia. The deep purple aconitum would make a wonderful combination with the delphinium, lime-green euphorbia, and lighter green hydrangea. Add peonies and phlox for scent.

1 *Stachys byzantina*
2 *Heuchera* 'Plum Pudding'
3 *Astrantia major* 'Claret'
4 *Catananche caerulea* 'Major '
5 *Aster* 'Sapphire'
6 *Aquilegia vulgaris* 'Nora Barlow'
7 *Salvia nemorosa* 'Caradonna'
8 *Echinops ritro* 'Veitch's Blue'
9 *Paeonia* 'Sarah Bernhardt'
10 *Aconitum carmichaelii* 'Arendsii'
11 *Sedum* 'Matrona'
12 *Echinacea* 'Green Envy'
13 *Campanula lactiflora*
14 *Polygonatum multiflorum*
15 *Aquilegia vulgaris* 'Ruby Port'
16 *Angelica gigas*
17 *Monarda* 'Beauty of Cobham'
18 *Aconitum carmichaelii* Wilsonii Group
19 *Phlox paniculata* 'Jade'
20 *Paeonia lactiflora* 'Monsieur Jules Elie'
21 *Phlox paniculata* 'Monica Lynden-Bell'
22 *Campanula lactiflora* 'Prichard's Variety'
23 *Hydrangea paniculata* 'Limelight'
24 *Delphinium* 'Blue Jay'
25 *Euphorbia wulfeniil*

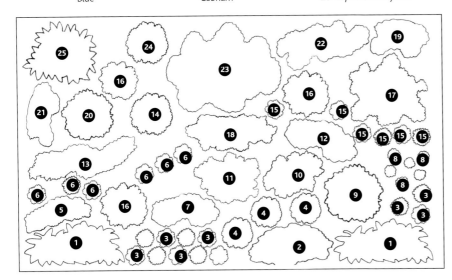

early summer

The garden comes into its own in the early summer. As we started this book in the fall, and worked throughout the year until the summer, the team that worked on it were surprised what wonders my bare patches of earth can produce when summer is truly upon us.

By the time we get to the early summer we are over our worries about late frosts, and every year the garden really comes into shape in the most magical way.

I have two distinct outdoor rooms in my garden, and purple alliums and irises dominate one at this time of year. When the stately flag irises zoom up from the corm you almost want to hang around and watch them unfold into stunning individual beauties. I find alliums very rewarding, as they reappear each year. Their foliage is a little annoying, as it can turn yellow quite quickly and makes the garden look untidy. But it is worth it for the length of the bloom and overall effect.

At this time of year I am always drawn to simple daisies. I like to do a dinner or lunch table arrangement using just this type of flower. The dainty feverfew daisies are so sweet, and I adore their slightly woody scent. They last amazingly well, too. I also love the wild ox eye daisies that line the countryside. This year I have planted *Leucanthemum* 'Aglaia' and 'Little Miss Muffet'.

The early summer is about the return of wonderful flowers such as my delicate poppies, blowsy peonies, and favorite roses. I have chosen my roses for scent and color, so I adore 'Gertrude Jekyll' and 'Constance Spry' for their gorgeous pink color and shape. The mid-pink 'Bonica' is also a good rose to cut. Early June sees my 'Rambling Rector' erupt into a mass of creamy-white blooms that saturate my arbors. This has a lovely myrrh scent that I sniff on my way out for a walk with the dogs. Another climbing rose that I revere in June is 'Alberic Barbier', and I have been training 'Pink Bells' down a wall with great success.

LEFT Our fascination with green flowers grows each year. These bright green *Dianthus barbatus* are like pompons of moss on a stem.

ABOVE Small marguerite daisies have such wonderful cushion centers of yellow. Their shaggy petals make you want to see if "he loves you" or not.

When I see the lupins nodding their heads with delphiniums and foxgloves, I know that summer is in full swing. It's about the salvias, cornflowers, and catmint all filling out the beds and hiding the earth for a few months, and the bees returning to spend time among the purple haze of my 'Hidcote' lavender.

OPPOSITE I am always looking for fun containers, and small ones like these keep down the cost and are ideal to dot up and down the table. Fresh yellow *Achillea* is such a wonderful intense color, seen here with marguerite daisies and feverfew.

breakfast alfresco Unless you are lucky enough to live in a part of the world blessed with year-round sunshine, having breakfast outside is such a rare treat that it deserves a good table decoration. What nicer way to start the day if you have guests staying for the weekend or want a treat to celebrate a summer birthday? These tiny arrangements were plucked from my garden, and you can see that there is a mix of flowers just going out of season, such as the wallflowers and bluebells, with early summer flowers coming into season, such as the alliums, herbs, and roses. If you are unsure whether the color combination of your selection will work, you can always add a little green to help out, especially a great lime color like the acidly sharp *Alchemilla mollis*.

THIS PAGE Tiny little ceramic flowerpots hold miniature hand-tied posies of garden finds. Some "weeds" have also been included, such as the forget-me-nots and the clover.

OPPOSITE When you clear the table after the meal, you can move the pots into the house with you to prolong your enjoyment.

pretty peonies

Peonies are always popular flowers, and you cannot beat a vase of peonies arranged simply on their own in the summer. In the garden I find them rather a short-lived flower and actually prefer them when cut. If you buy them fresh in bud they should last five to seven days, depending on the weather. The miracle of these flowers is how they progress from a round bud that resembles a sprout to such an ethereal beauty about seven times their original size. Of course, when they shatter they make a huge mess but, boy, that last day when they are all resplendent in their most glorious state is an immense joy. I dread the thought of the lovely peony becoming an all-year-round flower like the dear, reliable chrysanthemum or the carnation, as I could not bear to see this seasonal treasure rendered so common!

LEFT It is a trend at the moment to have collections of vases grouped together. Here, I used 'Red Charm' peonies massed with *Euphorbia* x *martinii* and *Dianthus barbatus*. I adore the green against the deep red. I also used some amazing tropical stems of the ric-rac cactus, *Selenicereus anthonyanus*, and a small pompon of *Dianthus barbatus* 'Will Red'.

OPPOSITE The single heads of peonies placed in small ceramic vases are highlighted with a decorative red wire detail.

candy colors

For a tea party in July I was motivated by this cake for an unusual color scheme. I believe any color combination is possible if you use the correct proportions and include some green. The table center of diagonal rows makes use of grouping to help dilute the choice of vibrant color. Using rows of flowers horizontally, vertically, or across a container always gives a more contemporary feel. It works very well when the container is also low or not very deep. Here I used a 2-inch tall Perspex purple tray. On the cake, the deep brown chocolate also diffuses the color slightly, and it is made mellower by the essential use of the lime-green soft balls of *Viburnum opulus*. Peonies not only work well on their own, but they are also enormously useful in mixed arrangements. The most ubiquitous peony is 'Sarah Bernhardt' and here she is the focal flower, the most important in both the table center and the cake top. To make a splendid over-the-top cake top, use a small glass ramekin dish and fill it with a large enough piece of floral foam so that it rises above the edge of the glass. For soft icing, which will not support the weight of glass, I often use the bottom of a white polystyrene drinking cup, also filled with foam to hold the flowers.

OPPOSITE This simple wreath was created by binding rose heads of the bright pink spray rose 'Lovely Lydia' onto a mossed frame with reel wire. This might seem extravagant, but the roses will dry out naturally and the wreath becomes a dried decoration that will last months. I make one in the summer and keep it on my door until fall.

ABOVE The flower heads at the base of the cake are only temporary decorations as they are not placed in water.

RIGHT *Salvia nemorosa* 'Caradonna', yellow *Achillea* 'Moonshine', lime-green *Viburnum opulus*, red *Achillea* 'Paprika', and rows of 'Sarah Bernhardt' pink peonies make this lively table arrangement.

accent plants Two of my summer treasures are the long arched stems of *Polygonatum*, or Solomon's seal, prized for its elegant bells, and the velvety silver foliage of *Stachys byzantina*, or lamb's ears, as it is affectionately known. Originally from Turkey, Armenia, and Iran, *Stachys* is now cultivated all over the world as an ornamental plant. It thrives well in poor soil and starts to flower in the late spring, but continues to be decorative throughout the summer. There are several cultivars, but two worth a mention are 'Big Ears', which has large leaves up to 10 inches long, and a low-growing variety that has been named after the famous flower arranger, 'Sheila Macqueen'. They all offer wonderful foliage for summer arrangements and hand-tied bouquets as their gray color looks very elegant and striking and complements the summer palette.

BELOW This fine-looking *Stachys byzantina* was tied to a metal basket with raffia. Floral foam holds 'Miss Delilah' phlox, 'Figaro Lavender' stocks, and purple summer asters. Stems of handsome leafless Solomon's seal were drawn across the design to show off their creamy white bells to maximum effect.

"Solomon's seal is such a stunning plant in the garden, but as the summer goes on the leaves dominate the lovely white flowers. To make the most of these elegant bells I removed the leaves, so that they can be enjoyed to their best advantage."

celebrating early summer

outdoor party

There is something so exquisite about being able to enjoy your garden by entertaining friends and family outdoors in the sun. Sadly, it is always a bit of a last-minute decision where I live in England, as the weather can be quite changeable and dull, even in the so-called summer!

However, there is no better way to dress an outdoor party than with the flowers, foliages, and herbs of the season. When I got married, I had just switched my career from a history teacher to florist and was wildly enthusiastic about my flowers. I was married at harvest time, so it seemed totally appropriate to include wheat in the flowers and foliage I selected for my wedding party. At this time of year I like to use barley, with its longer ears, and herbs such as lavender to line floral foam in the same way as I have made this arrangement. A similar effect can be achieved with straight twigs, such as dogwood, held into the foam with hair pins of strong florist wire, or lengths of equisetum or other reeds and grasses that grow well and are plentiful in the summer.

LEFT I pinned ears of wheat into a long block of floral foam to make a simple long summer table center. For the flowers I chose a mixture of herbs—bergamot and dill—combined with delphiniums, roses, and dahlias.

OPPOSITE The foam block is great for a long table as it is not too wide or too tall to get in the way of the food or conversation.

late summer

In late summer I am drawn to oranges, yellows, purples, and mixed colors, and I like to use vegetables and fruits in my decorations. I experiment more with bright color schemes, in an attempt to make the most of the colors of summer before the fall sets in.

By this time the hedges are starting to produce their berries, and early species like viburnums are fully formed. Small apples appear on the trees and are the perfect size to use in floral decorations. This is when fruit and vegetables are at their least expensive, so it makes economic sense to experiment with a few in your late summer arrangements.

As the summer is at its peak, all my herbaceous perennials are plump and tall in the border. They might be showing some signs of wear by this point—they are a little faded from the summer sun, have perhaps suffered the ravages of insects, an occasional downpour of rain, or sway of winds, but they are still undeniably attractive.

The spiky echinops and eryngium remain strong and lean. Agapanthuses—mostly in pots in my garden, as I have lost so many in harsh winters—are looking fine and elegant. I think these flowers are so inspirational, in the garden or in a vase. The late summer is the only time I can really seriously take gladioli to my heart. Now in their season, displayed en masse in a vase they can even appear stylish. At other times of the year, these hardworking

familiar spires are very functional for giving elevation and depth to a pedestal arrangement. But they are too stiff and they do not dance enough to make it into my garden! One flower that is the talk of the August garden is the *Agastache* family. This is a long-flowering perennial that everyone wants in their summer border because it is so floriferous. Commonly known as the giant hyssop, there is one favorite that deserves a mention. 'Black Adder' emerges dark purple, even black, and then turns to red and has a delicious scented foliage. It makes some tall vertical lines in the border.

In my herb garden I also still enjoy the self-seeding bronze fennel, *Foeniculum vulgare* 'Purpureum'. Another self-seeder who has mischievously appeared all over the place in my garden is silver dollars. However, I cannot be too harsh about *Lunaria annua*, as all flower arrangers love those seed heads.

For more vivid colors I turn to sunflowers, with some spires of orange *Croscosmia*. For smaller arrangements there are lots of daisy-shaped flowers, such as the heleniums that start to

ABOVE Lavender prefers to grow on its own rather than to compete with other plants, so I now have one stunning border where I allow this beautiful scented plant to dominate happily.

flower in June and are still flowering when the first frosts begin. Some of the stars of my summer though are my lily bulbs. I have several that survived being the decoration for a grand wedding and then ended up in my garden. They remind me of some of the wonderful places I have worked in and had the pleasure of decorating. Their scent also transports me back to my own wedding day.

"Arrangements consisting of one flower type in a vase are so simple and visually very effective. Make the most of the abundance of summer to achieve this full effect."

THIS PAGE Currently the *Matthiola incana* varieties of stocks are having a big revival, prized for their gorgeous scent by nearly all the top floral designers. It is one flower that I buy most often for my own home. I place ten stems in a vase in my bathrooms throughout the summer. It does not last long—by day five it starts to degrade and not look so lush and full. About this time they reveal their close relationship to the brassicas, and the gorgeous fragrance turns more to that of rotting cabbages!

hot colors

Late summer is a time for using the first fruits and berries and for enjoying some heat in the color of our flower arrangements. I like the combination of turquoise and orange. I became inspired by the use of the blue palette with orange after a trip to Portugal, where blue is used in so many of the tiles that feature in the architecture. At the end of summer there are lots of tall orange flowers to choose from, such as *Eremurus*, *Kniphofia*, *Crocosmia*, and gladioli.

THIS PAGE I like the way willow twists so I formed it into a screen tied with some turquoise aluminum wires. I twisted the *Kniphofia* following the way that they have grown. At the base, a long block of floral foam holds *Physocarpus* foliage with some roses, dahlias, *Crocosmia*, and a few small sprigs of blue delphinium.

Lime green and orange is another bright combination that I enjoy in the late summer. I usually add a touch of burgundy foliages for fillers, too. These solanum fruits often appear at the Dutch auctions and last surprisingly well in water. Harder than they look, they wire into decorations well. But be aware that all fruit and vegetables will shorten the life of your arrangements, because as they degrade they emit the ethylene gas that is the "grim reaper" to flowers!

THIS PAGE I used some orange solanums in a glass vase and filled it with lime-green *Alchemilla mollis*, the burgundy umbels of *Daucus carota* 'Dara', my favorite dill *Anethum graveloeons*, and the brown *Sanguisorba officinalis*, to give life to the Ecuadorian-grown 'Geisha' and 'Star 2000' roses.

picking for fragrance

lavender basket

From June to late August there is usually a good supply of cut lavender, and until it starts to drop, it makes a wonderful decoration for bunching and tying onto a metal frame or using double-sided tape for a glass or plastic container. This requires quite a lot of time and more lavender than you imagine!

1

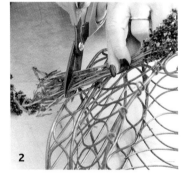

2

3

You will need

- a sturdy wire basket
- a block of floral foam
- 5 bunches of lavender
- 20 stems of *Alchemilla mollis*
- 20 stems of flowering mint
- 5 stems of *Eryngium* Sirius Questar
- 15 stems of *Leucanthemum* x *superbum* 'Wirral Supreme'
- 20 stems of garden roses
- 20 stems of *Scabious caucasica* 'Stafa'
- a few stems of clematis
- a few sweet peas
- a roll of ribbon or raffia
- scissors

1 Gather your materials. I used a wirework basket, but you can also use a wicker one, provided it has an open weave so you can tie in the lavender stems.

2 Divide your lavender into neat bunches. Trim some of the bunches so the flowers rise above the top of the basket. Tie in place with ribbon or raffia. Cut other bunches and place them onto the basket at different heights.

3 Continue until the whole basket is complete. Follow the shape of your chosen container— this one curves up to the handles—so that it looks well covered and has a lush effect.

4 Line the basket with some heavy plastic (we use garbage bags) and then place a block of foam in the center. You may need more than one, depending on the size of your basket, as you must make sure your block is as high as the top of the lavender to create the effect of a full basket.

5 Add the sprigs of *Alchemilla mollis* and then the flowering mint. Place every stem as if it is coming from the same central point of the arrangement. This gives a natural feel to the flowers.

6 Add the *Eryngium*. At this point you should not be able to see any of the green flower foam.

7 Add all the flowers, leaving those with weaker stems to the end. You will need to place your hand close to the foam and push in the stems very carefully.

celebrating late summer

rehearsal dinner

I think the rehearsal dinners after wedding rehearsals are some of the loveliest parties I am honored to be involved in. Everyone is reunited, the mood is always optimistic for the next day, family and friends are relaxed, and everything is fixed and ready after months of hard work.

The flowers for the night before should always be relaxed and should not upstage the flowers planned for the wedding. These simple arrangements from the garden use a mixture of garden roses with some flowering mint and *Alchemilla mollis*. Straight-sided 12-inch glass bowls are so versatile and perfect for the round tables so often used by caterers. The bowls can be lined with many things, but for this relaxed garden dinner we used petals for one, pink hydrangea heads for another, and some lavender arranged inside the glass. These arrangements were made by lining the bowls with plastic and then using well-soaked floral foam. If you often arrange your own flowers at home for events, then I recommend investing in these straight-sided bowls because they can be used in so many ways. They look great just with floating flowers and candles when the budget and time are stretched. Alternatively, you can fill them with fruits or nuts and place floral foam rings around them. They can be filled with a beautiful selection of seasonal fruits, or just one or two flowers to give color and scent. You could even plant them with summer flowers, such as geraniums, or pots of herbs.

"The trick to using mixed colors from your garden is to leave out any white, as it dilutes the effect of the color. Use some frothy foliage such as Alchemilla mollis or mint, and try to mix up the colors as much as possible, like shuffling a deck of cards!"

OPPOSITE The flower selection includes flowering mint, *Alchemilla mollis*, garden roses, pink hydrangea, and lavender. Each bowl was internally lined with a different type of flower from the garden—pink hydrangea, lavender, or rose petals.

THIS PAGE Your table linen should always reach to the floor for a party and include a top cloth. I love to use color in the undercloth but have starched white linen on the top to make the most of my mixed colored flowers. If you use all-white flowers, then I recommend a deeper color to show them off.

creating wedding flowers Every wedding is so individual now, and it really is about the personality of the couple. One recent trend is for families to get more involved in the practicalities, either hand-making the invitations or the table cards, helping with the flowers, or making the cake. I think this idea is lovely, and over the years we have helped lots of people to really get involved in the arrangement of their own wedding flowers. It is the one time you are going to push the budget, so it is great to be able to be hands-on for some of the aspects! The most popular wedding bouquet is an all-rose bouquet and this is the easiest to make yourself. Roses spiraled into a bouquet always photograph well and look good with almost any style of dress and wedding. I also like floral hair decorations for young bridesmaids, and this one was made in a very easy way. Almost like a daisy chain it won't last long, but it will be perfect for the ceremony. Flowergirls are notoriously hard on their flowers, often placing them on their heads, so a basket or bag is better for them as they can put them down for a rest more easily. Over the years we have covered plastic pots with velvet, floral prints, satin, silk, and even made bags out of plant materials.

ABOVE A simple classic bouquet of creamy garden roses and a few sprigs of *Sanguisorba officinalis* 'Pink Tanna' looks good with most styles of wedding dresses.

RIGHT This headdress was created in a very simple way using fishing line on some plaited grass. If you wanted to try this, I suggest taking some soft vines, such as ivy trails or jasmine, and making a circlet of the correct size for your flower girl or bridesmaid. Then snip some small heads of flowers, berries, and greenery and bind them onto the vines with some clear fishing line. I used some rue, honeysuckle, *Sanguisorba officinalis* 'Pink Tanna', and viburnum berries.

"Daisies look so fresh for a summer wedding and are perfect for flower girls. I grow Camille daisies in my herb garden and often buy the small Tanacetum *daisies commercially. 'Pure Kamille' is one of my favorites."*

Fall is one of my favorite seasons. The changes in the landscape bring a dramatic new color scheme and an array of plant material that is a unique inspiration in itself to the floral artist or nature lover.

fall

I love the mood of fall, the melancholy feeling that starts to descend when the days get shorter and the sun starts to lose its fire. I find myself in the mood for a little introspection and reflection. For the gardener it is the end of the growing cycle for that year, so we all pad around our garden congratulating ourselves on our triumphs and planning better strategies where our success has been less forthcoming. For me fall has always been the time for "turning over a new leaf," for making new plans for the new seasonal year. With the shortening days, our most productive part of the year is coming to a close. As soon as the leaves start to turn color and fall, I find my comfort in the bulb and seed catalogs as I plan my next cycle of growth. It's the perfect tonic pouring over the high color of next year's spring bulbs while everything in the landscape starts to fade. Once fall is underway we are exposed once more to the structures of our garden and landscape, and this is a time when evergreens start to come into their prime season. Shape and texture are more significant in fall and it is from these two areas that we can get most of our inspiration for indoor decoration. One of the key seasonal plants for me are rose hips. Each variety of rose produces very different hips and there is now a vast array on offer to the flower lover. Most rose nurseries also categorize their plants for fall seed head color as well as for their summer blooms. Hips come in all shapes and sizes, from the size of a pea up to the size of a small tomato. They start green and then develop into an amazing array of colors, from pink, yellow, and orange to deep red. Two varieties that are popular for their hips are *Rosa rugosa*, which makes a great wild hedge, and *Rosa* 'Pumpkin', which has orange hips that are great for decorations for Halloween and Thanksgiving.

RIGHT Rose hips are the new "must-have" filler for fall arrangements. For many years now they have been playing a support role as one of my favorite fillers for fall bouquets and arrangements, but now they are moving into the center stage and becoming the stars of the show.

what's good in the garden

For me the fall garden is one of extremes, full of deep, rich, and bright colors. This is the time of year when I am not drawn at all to the classic combination of white and green. I want rich schemes and a flash of color before the onslaught of winter. The colors are fiery reds, yellows, oranges, and browns or purple and burgundy.

The fall border has some very showy flowers, such as sunflowers and erect gladioli, as well as some very delicate flowers I adore that are native to the North American prairies. Rudbeckia, echinacea, and heleniums have a long flowering period and are essential for the flower arranger as they also last well as a cut flower. Heleniums are a good garden and vase flower. In fact, if you cut them back at the end of summer, they will reward you with new blooms for your vases in October.

I adore the umbrella shapes of the celery family, such as the seed heads of wild dills and parsley, and the seed heads of eryngium and astrantia. These fillers mix well with the last rose blooms, rose hips, and the final dazzling flowers of the fall. Flashy dahlias, elegant nerines, stately aconitum, and chrysanthemums are among my favorites to pick from the garden at this time. Odd heads of helenium and a few sunflowers, straggling heads of brightly colored achillea mixed with dill, are always favorite combinations for my kitchen table.

OPPOSITE Sedum is a useful filler. I love its texture and the wonderful succulent leaves. I am growing several varieties in my garden, and this year I am taken by the delicate nature and burgundy color of 'Ruby Glow'. 'Vera Jameson' has pink fluffy heads in fall on the gorgeous beetroot stems.

ABOVE RIGHT Purple, pink, and lime green make one of my favorite color combinations, so at this time of year I like to mix the carmine pink *Aster novae-angliae* 'Andenken an Alma Pötschke' with spires of purple aconitum and *Gladiolus* 'Green Star'.

FAR RIGHT Dogwood comes into its own in this season, when the color of the stems takes over as the leaves start to turn brown and fall off. Now there is very little in the garden that is green so the yellow stems of *Cornus stolonifera* 'Flaviramea' are more arresting in the fall landscape.

RIGHT The perennial wallflower *Erysimum* 'Bowle's Mauve' is less familiar than its annual relatives, but this quiet plant with its lilac flowers on a short woody shrub is particularly tenacious, flowering right through fall into the winter.

OPPOSITE From the end of the summer until Christmas, I use *Malus* in my decorations and arrangements. I adore crab apples and sometimes use full-size apples in larger vases. We wire them into arrangements and then hang them onto garlands and wreaths at Christmas.

CLOCKWISE FROM TOP LEFT *Verbena bonariensis* provides useful height in the border and in vases and arrangements. It can be damaged by heavy frosts, as it is only borderline hardy. To help protect it, do not cut it right back in the fall but leave it until the spring when new growth is in evidence.

Dill is one of my favorite fillers. I love the shape, color, and smell of *Anethum graveolens*. The yellow flat umbels give a light natural feel to arrangements, and the foliage is so delicate.

Nigella, seen here among orange marigolds, is a quintessential cottage garden flower. Its seed heads are almost as interesting as the flowers.

Scabiosa columbaria var. *ochroleuca* is one of those flowers that transports me back to my childhood.

I have been converted to using heucheras in the last few years. I love color and these little plants, mainly grown for their foliage, come in an amazing array. *Heuchera* 'Peach Flambé' is very gaudy, but that is what this season needs!

Tall, elegant, and with the bonus of movement, miscanthus plays a fantastic supporting role to flowers both in the garden and in a vase arrangement.

what's good to buy

In the stores and the flower markets there is still an abundance of flowers available, with dahlias and chrysanthemums being the most plentiful. They are the best buy because they are in season and they really do last well. Both have a huge variety of colors and shapes, so we can all find something we like.

If we take the often-maligned chrysanthemum, there has to be one that you can take to your heart and adore! Even if you only ever buy white flowers, use the white daisy variety, which is pure and simple and makes a lovely display with some grasses or herbs in an old milk pitcher. I like to float a single standard chrysanthemum head in a medium-sized fish bowl, with the base of the bowl filled with crab apples. This simple but effective use of one flower and some abundant plant material makes a modern arrangement. Three of these down a long table give you a stunning table decoration in less than five minutes. Even the double varieties of chrysanthemums, traditionally used for sympathy tributes, can be given the contemporary twist. I have toned down bright yellow double chrysanthemums with fall leaves. This is also the prime time for grasses in the garden and also for seed heads and fruits.

LEFT Double spray chrysanthemums, such as these rich red 'Quinty', can be found really inexpensively at farmers' markets or nurseries at this time of year, so you can afford to buy them in large quantities.

ABOVE RIGHT *Astrantia* 'Roma' has an ethereal quality. It has a long season in the garden and is grown increasingly around the world as a delicate filler for flower designs.

Coneflower is the common name for *Echinacea purpurea*. This light brown variety, from which the petals have been stripped, is 'White Swan'.

1 The rich squashy berries of the guelder rose are like clusters of red currants.

2 The colorful orange berries of *Auranticarpa rhombifolia* resemble tiny pumpkins.

3 *Helianthus annuus*, the common sunflower, is a tower of sunshine at the end of the summer. It looks great as a single flower or massed with some dill and a few stems of *Cotinus*.

4 'Cassandra' is one of the most popular cut flower varieties of aster. This small lilac daisy is fast growing and gives a good return to the grower as well as being an extremely long-lasting cut flower in all arrangements.

5 *Chrysanthemum* 'Princess Armgard Red' is popular with growers throughout the world.

6 *Brassica oleracea* 'Red Crane' is also referred to as flowering kale. The purple 'Crane Pink' and 'White Crane' varieties are also widely grown in fall and winter.

7 Grasses are one of the trendiest fall fillers. *Panicum* 'Fountain' is prized for its textural interest.

8 This red rose hip is *Rosa* 'Amazing Fantasy'. In the Netherlands and Italy, growers are seeing the commercial value of the hip and the acreage given over to their cultivation increases each year.

The abundant green seed heads of millet grass are used as an important food and feed crop in many parts of the world. It is also increasing in its popularity as foliage for flower arrangements. Particularly useful in vases and hand-tied bouquets, it adds movement to a design.

THIS PAGE After you have removed the suckers on apple trees you need to look for any dead wood and cut it out with a diagonal cut. Cut back crossing branches to allow wind to circulate—this helps the tree to be more disease resistant. Cut back all stems by about half to promote flowering and growth.

pruning fruit trees

When fall has arrived and winter is not far away, it is time to prune in the garden. It is best to get on with this before the frosts start, so before you have to scrape the frost off your windscreen in the mornings, you need to get out in the garden and start to edit!

The skies might be gloomy and the sun finding it hard to get above the hills, but most gardeners find that tidying up their garden is a real tonic to the spirits. Dead head the hydrangeas, cut back your roses, and trim back unruly bushes or vines. All deciduous trees benefit from being pruned at this time of year. Evergreens should be pruned in the early summer after their growth spurt. Trees that bloom in the spring will already have their blossom buds for the next year, so you have to be careful with any spring bloomers, such as cherry and apple blossom and lilacs. I always think it is a great time to see the bare bones of your garden, so I heavily prune my figs, which tend to grow a lot each summer. I also cut back my cotinus when I can still use its lovely burgundy leaves. Think of pruning as a regular haircut rather than surgery. It is a good time to restore shape to plants, tidy up unruly plants, and remember—they will always grow back! The bonus, too, for the flower arranger is storing all the interesting pieces for later use in flower arrangements, either left natural or with a lick of spray-paint at Christmas!

bulb planting

Bulb planting in the fall for me is split into two areas: mass planting of narcissus, tulips, and other bulbs in the garden to complement my spring borders and pots, and those bulbs bought to force for indoor flowering throughout the winter.

Amaryllis are originally from the tropics, so they need to be grown inside, away from frosts. Their bulbs are huge and the long green stems support a most majestic bloom. As their heads are enormous, with as many as four florets making one large flower mass, they generally need stalking for support. If you are going to try to grow bulbs in water you need vases that support the bulb at the top so the roots can trail down. They need to be stored in a cool dark place for around four weeks to encourage root growth.

Narcissus are the easiest to plant for Christmas gifts because you can plant some as late as mid-November and they will be looking and smelling fantastic just five weeks later. *Narcissus* 'Ziva' is one of my favorites; with its multiple fragrant, pure white heads it suits any interior.

Hyacinths are available in two categories: those that are prepared for indoor forcing and those that are intended to be planted directly into the garden.

LEFT Forced hyacinths are harvested earlier and subjected to different temperatures. If you plant them in mid-September and store them in a cool place for around nine weeks, you can force them to flower in about three weeks. After flowering, replant them in your garden, ready for the following spring.

herb garden

For the fall planting plan I consulted Jekka McVicar, who has an award-winning organic herb nursery in the west of England. She has written many successful books on growing and using herbs and is a guru on this vast topic.

Bay is such a useful and lovely fragrant foliage, and myrtle is an excellent herb both for culinary use or flower decoration. It has traditionally been the choice for royal wedding bouquets and makes a useful evergreen shrub in any herb garden. Bronze fennel is a striking flower in the herb border and works so well as a filler with mixed arrangements. I adore the aniseed smell of this aromatic herb. Thyme is a useful herb as it adds scent and color, even in the depths of winter. A few different evergreen perennial varieties are a must, and this is such a useful herb in the kitchen, too. *Papaver somniferum* is a truly beautiful plant and an excellent nectar source for bees. Daisies always have a special place in my heart, and feverfew is wonderful to look at or to take as an infusion.

1 *Laurus nobilis*
2 *Myrtus communis*
3 *Ammi visnaga*
4 *Foeniculum vulgare* 'Purpureum'
5 *Rosmarinus officinalis*
6 *Tanacetum parthenium*
7 *Origanum* 'Rosenkuppel'
8 *Salvia officinalis* 'Purpurascens'
9 *Papaver somniferum* Paeoniflorum Group
Flowers'
10 *Thymus vulgaris*
11 *Thymus* 'Fragrantissimus'
12 *Petroselinum crispum*

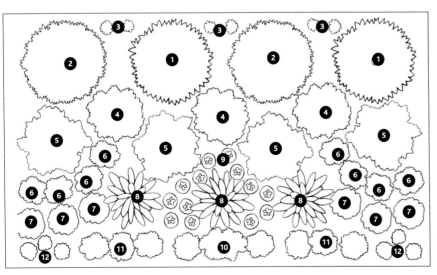

early fall

For as long as I have been arranging flowers, fruits and vegetables have been part of my palette, especially in the early fall when the landscape has an abundance of wonderful produce. The onset of fall also calls us out for woodland walks to admire the gifts of the forest.

Even when I was based in the city, I would take inspiration from woodland walks on Hampstead Heath or even one of the grand London parks such as St. James'. Early morning trips to the fruit and vegetable markets would also provide the stimulus for designs and ideas.

The *Malus* genus is one of the most versatile, useful, and inexpensive fall fruits. From huge cooking apples to small ornamental crab apples, they can enhance displays through texture and color. For a long time flower arrangers have known the value of lime green to enhance an arrangement and the addition of one or two 'Granny Smith' green apples

has the same effect. A rosy red apple gives a rich and vibrant tone to an arrangement, and small crab apples are excellent for tall pedestals and vases as well as wreaths.

The fall is a great time to celebrate black. I adore the juicy pointed berries of the *Ligustrum* genus and the black berries of *Viburnum tinus*, which look like they have been coated with blue enamel. The bramble genus also works well in flower arrangements and hand-tied bouquets, if you wear your gardening gauntlets! Another spiky black berry that is common in the hedges in my garden is the sloe. Useful for flavoring gin, it also makes a long-lasting cut branch. The shapes of the branches are often very asymmetrical, so I love to use them in a simple display with late aconitum or hydrangea.

One of the reasons I adore fall is it gives me an excuse to use more color and particularly to enjoy the more vibrant colors in the spectrum. The fading light levels make us naturally drawn to the warmer, richer colors of

LEFT Apples are so useful to the flower arranger. They come in a range of colors and sizes, are much less expensive than flowers, and add texture.

ABOVE Sedum is a lovely rose-colored flower that provides flowers for cutting from August to October. It turns brown with age and still looks wonderful.

nature, and as our mood turns to heavier choices for food, so does our taste for color and heavier decorations.

My work throughout the year is always inspired by texture, but never more so than in this season. I think the deeply toned foliages and berries also allow us to be more adventurous in our use of color combinations. I adore the breadth of choice available in fall, when we start to use nuts, fruits, and seed heads as well as vegetables and twigs.

THIS PAGE There is something lovely about seeing the purple sloes in the hedge at this time of year, and although this plant can be spiky it works well in a vase and holds its fruits. An asymmetrical arrangement was inspired by the shape of this branch, simply adorned with five huge heads of *Hydrangea macrophylla* 'Bela'.

wrapping vases

Long before recycling became such an important part of our daily lives, I always thought the wrapping of leaves around a simple glass jar made something magical out of the garbage! All you need is some double-sided tape and some leaves. I usually buy my tape from a hardware store, as double-sided carpet tape is usually quite wide and is perfect for leaves. At this time of year, you can literally pick the leaves off the ground and place them around an old jam jar. Add a hand-tied bouquet or even just one single large fall bloom, such as a standard chrysanthemum or a dahlia, or another favorite—a single sunflower. As a simple idea it looks better repeated—I usually make an odd number such as three, or five if I am feeling generous. My favorite leaves to use from my garden are laurel, rhododendron, large ivy leaves, sycamore, or oak. Herbs are also perfect, and all year round I make rosemary pots from my long rosemary hedge that is the length of my herb patch. Of course, with double-sided tape you can use anything from newspaper to fabric, or even colored card or gift-wrapping paper. It gives a new look to a simple small container and the overall effect is always good.

BELOW Black cordyline leaves were tied around some tumblers with ribbon and lace to give a vintage feel. Groups of rose hips, *Viburnum tinus* berries, and astrantia were arranged with 'Pepita' spray roses.

THIS PAGE The last of the summer 'Gertrude Jekyll' roses were used with Germini 'Kinky', *Ajania pacifica* 'Yellowday', the commercial *Rosa* 'Apricot', and a weed, known as penny cress to many, which is now being cultivated as the cut flower *Thlaspi perfoliatum* 'Green Bell'. Black leaves were tied around the tumblers with ribbon and wire threaded with pearls. These leaves are known in the trade as "black tea" leaves but they are really the 'Black Magic' cultivar of *Cordyline fruticosa*. The flat leaves have a central spine and are between 12 and 24 inches long. They are available throughout the year and are prized for their dark color, which can often have lighter magenta stripes in the center.

sculptural arrangements

Being restrained in color, or using just one variety of flower, is always a way of making an arrangement more striking. Making something grand but simple is what I strive for with my arrangements. Living topiary has long been a trademark design of mine, and they always look good and work in most environments. The fall is a good time to make them, using sunflowers, agapanthus seed heads, or even bunches of grasses. Tower arrangements are another modern device for making an economical arrangement look more spectacular. One of my favorite flowers to use for this design is the calla lily, as it is such an elegant flower.

THIS PAGE Fall is a time to look at the structure of the landscape and the garden and to appreciate topiary shapes. I have always enjoyed tying seasonal flowers together at the base of their heads to make "living topiary." Here, bunches of the foxtail millet *Setaria italica* 'Tomer' were bound together and placed in a blue glass vase in water. I added a little moss to the sides of the bunch to keep it upright. As a side detail, a small head of green hydrangea was added to a patterned drinking glass.

THIS PAGE Less is more when you are putting together a sculptural arrangement. To exaggerate height, these orange chrysanthemum heads on long stems were bound together at successive intervals with twine. The only other component is a single stem of orange rose hips.

grouping flowers Creating small hand-tied bouquets is a simple way to make the most of the last of your garden flowers. By grouping you can have a huge mix of color and add imperfect or weather damaged blooms in bunches. You can use seed heads such as these petal-less sunflowers for texture, while sprigs of fall grasses add a little movement to the chunky fall flowers. These 6-inch cubes are my favorite vases because they are the perfect size for coffee tables and dining tables. The neat size of the vase leaves plenty of room for food platters and glasses so you can entertain "family style" but still have lovely table decorations. In the fall in particular, I like to use vases of flowers mixed with some full of fruits or nuts. Here, I used a line of the same vases to create a long and narrow table center display; I used cob nuts, red-hot chili peppers, and wet walnuts to fill the other vases. The idea is very versatile and can be adapted with cones, seed heads, or store cupboard ingredients such as star anise or cinnamon sticks. It also works very well for children's parties, when you can fill the spare vases with wrapped chocolates or candies.

THIS PAGE Vibrantly colored bunches were created by grouping together flowers and foliages to create a rich textural effect. Grasses, sage, and ivy berries are the base for these garden flowers. Petal-less sunflowers and rudbeckia add texture to bright red, pink, and burgundy dahlias, Japanese anemones, and *Verbena bonariensis*, while fountain grass adds movement to the chunky flower heads.

using herbs from your garden

rosemary

The fragrance and the color of this useful evergreen herb make it one of my favorites. I include it in tied bunches, but I like to make an arrangement more sculptural either by placing it around a jar or vase with double-sided tape or, as here, by pinning it into floral foam.

1

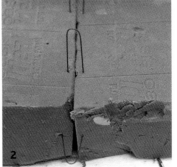

2

4

5

You will need

- a flat glass platter
- 2 blocks of standard floral foam
- a large bunch of cut rosemary
- 20 stems of multicolored aster daisies
- a few heavy stub wires
- a sharp knife

1 Cut the floral foam to fit the glass dish using a knife, allowing equal space all around. You will probably need to use two larger pieces and cut them to size. Make sure you keep the cut sides as straight as possible.

2 Secure the two blocks together by creating a hair pin from a length of stub wire and pin the two blocks firmly together.

3 Bundle together some similarly sized pieces of rosemary; place a heavy stub wire through the center and then twist the two ends of the wire together to form a neat bunch.

4 Place the bundles upright around the edge of the foam and pin them in place with the ends of the wire. Make sure the rosemary is at least 2 inches above the floral foam. Continue until you have completed the square and covered all sides of the floral foam.

5 Check for any gaps where you can see the foam through the rosemary bundles and fill with extra rosemary if necessary.

6 Trim the rosemary so that it is neat and all at one level so the arrangement does not look too dumpy and flat.

7 Push the asters into the foam in a horizontal grid, with the flower heads ahigher than the rosemary. Keep the foam moist and make sure there is enough water on the platter to keep the rosemary fresh.

"The trick here is to buy a few exotic, brightly colored flowers and mix with lots of inexpensive seasonal flowers and foliage to create a vibrant design!"

long-lasting luxury Sometimes it is hard to make a rich combination from the garden alone and we need to buy a few gorgeous flowers to mix with inexpensive seasonal flowers to create a visual design. Gerbera are always available and come in an astonishing array of colors. Here I have used the small Germini *Gerbera* 'Scream' and matched it to some *Celosia* 'Bombay Purple'. The inspiration for this purple-pink combination was the heather that I used to make the container. Inspiration comes from many sources. As well as the natural world I am particularly drawn to textiles and ribbons, and when I found a lampshade designer who produced custom-made lampshades using ribbon, I immediately adapted the idea to vases. The gloriosa lily, with its flame pink and yellow petals and lime-green buds, has long been a muse from the natural world for my designs.

OPPOSITE This rich mix includes *Celosia* 'Bombay Purple, Germini *Gerbera* 'Scream', *Leonotis leonurus*, combined with *Physalis alkekengi*, the burgundy *Dahlia* 'Arabian Night', ivy berries, and the pink snowberry *Symphoricarpos* from my garden. A plastic container was wrapped in double-sided tape and then covered with sprigs of purple heather. Halved eggplants were then cut to slide over the edges of the pot.

RIGHT Exotic pink and green celosia, groups of rich colored roses, textural orange pin cushion proteas, and just a few stems of precious gloriosa were added to the seasonal flowers. Groups of rose hips nestle against orange carthamnus, while bundles of ivy and hypericum berries add structure. The stripy containers are ribbon lampshades filled with glass cylinders.

"This table design is a perfect example of how to make something grand out of inexpensive flowers and a very natural design—this looks like fall leaves scattered on the ground."

THIS PAGE A simple table center was created using a bunch of yellow double chrysanthemum with some dried heads of *Scabiosa stellata* and a few oak leaves. The flower heads are not in water, so after dinner, I suggest recutting the stems and floating them in a low bowl to create a further, longer-lasting arrangement.

a harvest supper

The harvest festival is always an important time to decorate your local church and school, or to give thanks for the abundant harvest whatever your religious beliefs. Harvest is from the Anglo-Saxon word "haerfest" that literally translates as "fall." Wreaths are popular for Halloween and Thanksgiving, so it is a good idea to make a long-lasting wreath that will welcome all to your house over several months.

1

2

You will need

- 6 feet heavy vine—grape vine or clematis is good
- a few bunches of different colored peppers
- a box of dried maize, or corn cobs
- a ball of heavy-duty decorative string or raffia
- wire cutters and scissors
- a reel of heavy stub wire
- a length of ribbon

1 First, make the vine into a wreath shape by binding the vines together. Next, trim the peppers into small bunches and prepare with a tie. Also add some ties to the dry tufty ends of the maize. Attach stub wires to each piece.

2 Add the prepared bunches to the wreath in groups using the stub wire, working around the vine. Finally, add the ribbon to the top through the vine so that it makes a secure loop to hang the ring.

late fall

As the winter approaches there is far less in our gardens to pick from. Our designs often become more minimalist and creative to make the most of the foliage, seed heads, and late flowers we can harvest from the garden to go with our purchased flowers.

While the leaves might have disappeared from the trees and bushes, there are still rose hips and berries to be used. In my garden I have planted *Callicarpa* because it has the most stunning, almost iridescent, purple berries. I use them in tall displays, and sometimes I float the berries with candles and the odd dahlia flower that I can still find in the garden in a water-filled bowl.

Apart from the newly undressed willow and hazel, I am a huge fan of the dogwood species that cheer up our gardens with their colorful bare branches. The other great treasures of the fall are the catkins of the alder and the hazel. The alders have the elongated male catkins still intact, which resemble small cones and often get confused with mulberries. These relaxed and bendy branches are fantastic for working into rings and using in harvest wreaths. The climbing varieties of roses often produce some lovely long stems of rose hips, which look very elegant in bottles or vases and look stunning submerged under water with crab apples. From the vegetable patch you may find some brassica that have gone to seed, or you

can buy some of the cut varieties that are now widely available throughout the fall. These make good fillers or focal flowers. Use a drop of bleach in the water or tablets sold for sterilizing babies' bottles to avoid them making the water too smelly.

Also great at this time of year are the seed heads of the *Cynara scolymus*, or artichoke flowers. The variety 'Cardy' is a bright purple thistle that needs tall vases as the branches can rise to 6 feet. I also like to use blackberries in my arrangements at this time of year, although to be honest I do like the thornless varieties you can buy at the Dutch auction, which we often mix with stems of chili peppers. One capsicum that is worth a mention is the black bobbly 'Black Giant', which is perfect for Halloween.

Fruits of the *Cucurbita* genus, of which the pumpkin is a giant member, are also fun to use in the fall. The bright orange colors and markings of gourds are one of those seasonal joys I always cherish. Gourds look attractive but are not very tasty, so they are grown for their decorative uses. They are ready to harvest when the colors are at their most intense and the skin

ABOVE These beech and oak leaves are just on the turn, when they still have some green in them, and some are holding onto the stem.

is thick and tough. Make sure you bring them indoors before the first frosts. Skewer them into arrangements with bamboo canes, or just enjoy them arranged together in a bowl.

THIS PAGE 'Golden Delicious' apples, echinacea seed heads, rosemary, sage, white nerines, a few stems of miscanthus grass, hips, and some *Malus* were used to create this very natural flower table center. The low glass bowl was filled with fall leaves and wet floral foam to anchor the flowers. Twigs or kebob sticks can be used to anchor the apples.

"Late fall treasures! I planted this sunny yellow-petaled echinacea in my garden because I love the combination of its green cone against the soft petals, and they look equally good in arrangements that celebrate the colors of the season."

creative ways with cornus

Since the seventeenth century, the thirty or fifty varieties of cornus have been commonly known as dogwood. Cornus is an unassuming and even dull bush when in leaf during the summer. It bears pale, usually white, flowers in early summer that are pretty, but when in foliage it is rarely used in floral arrangements. Some varieties also bear fruit or berries in the fall, which are decorative in the garden. However, it has long been prized for its strong and pliable stems that have been used for centuries to weave into baskets, tool handles, and walking canes. It is the stems and the structure of the plant that makes it irresistible and indispensable to the modern florist.

In landscaping it is viewed as a strong and useful plant and it is often planted on exposed sites where dogwood stand up to vandalism and neglect quite well. However, it is in the fall when the leaves drop from the trees that these "ugly duckling" plants have their moment and emerge as the swans of the garden. The beautiful and diverse hues of their stems add texture and color to the barren landscape. It is also during the fall or spring, with the fall or rise of the sap, that the stems are at their most pliable and useful to the flower arranger.

OPPOSITE, FAR LEFT
Planted in great masses the bold stems of the red dogwood are used to striking effect in gardens. 'Sibirica' has the most vibrant scarlet stems. All straight-stemmed cornus should be planted in groups of five or seven, in a place where the winter sunlight slants through the thickets. Both *Cornus alba* 'Aurea' and 'Sibirica Variegata' have gorgeous red stems. *Cornus alba* 'Kesselringii' has striking black-purple stems. I grow a few of each in groups and prune heavily in February to promote good colored stems the following year.

OPPOSITE, LEFT To aid flower arranging dogwood can be woven, twisted, or used structurally.

THIS PAGE Red dogwood was used in the base of the vase as well as in the design of the flowers. Laid vertically and horizontally it creates visual interest. Orange Germini gerberas, red 'Tamango' spray roses, and green hanging amaranthus were used with glycerined beech leaves from Italy to create a simple fall coffee table arrangement.

elegant table center I adore boat-shaped vases as they make very versatile table centers. The problem is that they are often quite large and sometimes need masses of flowers to fill them, which can prove to be rather expensive. The trick is to use some spare plant material—stems of foliage in this case—as a framework and incorporate a smaller number of flowers. This type of arrangement is perfect for this time of year as it plays to the strengths of the season. Here, I used a frame of contorted willow and then placed rose hips and echinacea seed heads throughout.

LEFT The willow was bent into pleasing curves, secured with a little twine, and placed in the zinc boat. This then acts as an anchor for the flowers as well as providing a visible framework. It is functional and decorative.

BELOW Echinacea and rose hips secured with ribbon complete simple napkin ties that make the table look dressed, but in a casual, relaxed way.

season of mellow fruitfulness

ring of red

This simple wreath is straightforward to make and the materials are easy to procure. You can make the base from straw or hay, or green moss if you have enough. At this time of year moss is not too hard to find in gardens—either in patches on north-facing roofs or in grass. If you do remove it from the grass, you will improve your lawn at the same time!

1

2

You will need

- a wire coat hanger
- a bag of hay or straw
- a bag of moss
- 3 baskets of crab apples
- 20 stems of plump red hips
- heavy reel wire
- some short lengths of stub wire
- wire cutters and scissors
- a length of ribbon

1 Make a small wreath frame by bending a wire coat hanger into a ring and cutting off the hanging handle. Pack around the wire with hay or moss and bind tightly onto the frame with reel wire. Wire the moss onto the front of the ring in the same way. Next, prepare the crab apples by pushing a stub wire into the base, retaining the stalk.

2 Next, take some chunky rose hips and detach them from their stems. Wire through the hip using reel wire to make a long, continuous necklace of hips.

3 Push the crab apples into place on the front and sides of the wreath using the stub wires. Then loop the necklace of hips around the wreath, passing through the center of the ring. Fix the end of the wire at the back of the wreath. Finally, loop a length of the ribbon through the original wire frame at the back to attach your ring.

3

THIS PAGE These tall fluted glass vases can be used in a variety of ways and are very versatile. I adore using them with long Italian hips in the fall, and then filling them with crab apples. The simple hand-tied bouquet is made from fall garden hydrangea, hypericum, and the seed heads of scabious. The hydrangea and the scabious could be left to dry naturally, and you could reuse this arrangement with the addition of fresh greenery.

raiding your flower borders

natural bouquet

I love to adapt my own containers to make my flower arrangements look more natural and sculptural. Small wire baskets are perfect for this, and we often use the basket many times each season, adapted for different looks for weddings and other celebratory events. Here, it is filled with inexpensive flowers such as chrysanthemums and ornamental cabbages, and with some more expensive blooms such as hydrangea.

1

2

3

4

5

6

You will need

- a sturdy, loosely woven round basket
- 3 bunches of dried wheat
- some moss
- a selection of fall flowers
- several lengths of raffia
- wire cutters and scissors
- a glass vase or container
- a length of oasis bind wire

1 First, make about 24 bunches of 4 or 5 wheat flower heads tied with raffia. Place these around the basket by tying into place so all the ears of grain are about the same height and they look like

they are growing naturally. When you have completed the container, line it with moss and place a glass container in the center so you can fill it with water and flower food.

2 Now you are ready to make the hand-tied bouquet. Place all the plant material in groups of the same flower and strip the lower half of the stem by removing the leaves and stray branches.

3 Taking one central flower and a piece of foliage, place one piece to the left, and continue until you have placed 5 pieces into the arrangement. Then twist it in your hand and place another 5. Continue until you have added all the plant material.

4 At this point all the stems should be spiraled in the same direction and the top of the bouquet should be round and domed. The place where you have been holding the bunch is the binding point—secure at this position with the oasis bind wire.

5 Tie round the binding point with raffia as tightly as you can without damaging the stems.

6 Recut the stems with a diagonal cut then check that the arrangement fits neatly into the container in the center of the basket. Cut through the oasis bind wire and give a little shake to release the bunch slightly within its raffia tie.

THIS PAGE Simply cut pumpkins and gourds complement this undemanding and uncomplicated vase of contorted willow, hips, and apples. This arrangement is long lasting—if not kept too near the fire for long!

BELOW You can make a stunning, colorful arrangement that will impress your trick-or-treaters at Halloween from simple bunches of flowers and candy treats from your local supermarket.

celebrating late fall

halloween

There is no time like Halloween to celebrate the vegetable as an interior decoration. There are now such great varieties of pumpkins available—they are surely one of the sexiest and best-looking vegetables.

Pumpkins are wonderfully curvaceous, and by growing several varieties you can get some of the loveliest colors. The verdigris-skinned varieties, such as 'Queensland Blue' and 'Crown Prince', look fabulous next to the pale tangerine 'Munchkin' or the salmon pink 'Giant Pink Banana'. I also like the twisted gourds and the Turk's head varieties that are definitely more decorative than they are tasty! I adore using pumpkins with dahlias as they reach their peak together in a celebration of all that is abundant, fecund, and mature. Fall is the perfect time for celebrating the beauty and bounty of the harvest.

Halloween offers the ideal opportunity to decorate our homes with a sense of humor and eat lots of candy! The simple sweets and flower arrangement can be attempted easily after a trip to the supermarket. Pick your colored candies and then select flowers to match. I chose a cheap version of jelly beans and then one bunch of brightly colored roses, mixed with some solidaster and a bunch of foliage. Then I selected two bunches of complementary-colored chrysanthemums. One was the daisy 'Red Reagan' variety and the other the spiky yellow spider chrysanthemum.

Winter is dominated by textures and delights in foliage like no other season. Foliage plants become the stars of floral design at this time of year, and we value the evergreens for their fortitude in withstanding the cruel winds and low temperatures outside so we can bring them indoors to enjoy.

winter

The dreary cold winter months, with low levels of light and short days, can be filled with the wonder of taking plant material from the landscape and bringing the outside in. Add to this some spray paint, glitter, candles, and some seasonal fruits and nuts and you have the makings of a winter wonderland. For the professional florist, this season is the busiest. The fashioning of large decorations for shops, restaurants, offices, and homes can be very time consuming. Bags of moss and bundles of greenery are sought, to be bound together in garlands and topiaries to delight and fulfill fantasies. There is a lot of hidden support involved. Fruits, cones, spices, ribbons, and other decorative items all require heavy wiring before they can be maneuvered into the decorations of the season. Lighter decorations can make use of the hot glue gun, but any decoration that needs to be hung requires wiring and the structural engineering of a seasoned florist! The smell of the pine, the wet bracken texture of the moss, and the scent of cinnamon and star anise are enlivening and motivating at the start of the season, but by the end the dry chapped hands make one's enthusiasm wane slightly! However, the wonderful thing about the winter is that you can let your imagination lead your designs, and you can be more daring than at any other time of year. You can take the same plant material each year but create very different looks by varying the spray paint and the ribbon, and theme your event with an individual twist. Even the choice of gold or silver creates a very different effect: gold makes everything warmer and silver makes it colder.

RIGHT The variegated holly *Ilex aquifolium* 'Argentea Marginata' makes a good hedge or fine specimen plant for the winter garden. I have several standard plants. This is a female variety—if you want your holly to produce red berries, plant a male plant nearby to aid pollination. It is recommended that for every five female plants there is one male pollinator.

what's good in the garden

For three seasons the evergreens play a supporting role in the garden, but in the winter they get all the medals for the shape and color they give to the cold landscape. The evergreen plants give life to the garden when all the other plants have died down or lost their leaf.

I like to have at least a third of my garden with some color in winter, and I have my favorites. I adore box and *Ligustrum* for their structure. The large leaves of rhododendrons are fabulous in large arrangements or for using around tumblers and jelly jars. Pine and spruce are invaluable for making swags, garlands, and wreaths. I like larch for its fine fronds of foliage and fabulous cones. Living in England, I would find it hard to go through the winter without ivy, and I do miss this foliage when I am working in an area of the world that is devoid of this invasive and tenacious plant. Some herbs are also indispensable, such as rosemary and laurel, and the silver gray of lavender.

Although the weather might be bleak, by the end of the winter season there are some real stars that start to appear through the hard soil. One of the bravest and first to bloom is the delicate snowdrop. Its fragile appearance belies an exceptional hardiness; the leaves and flowers pierce the frozen topsoil and resist frost to be one of the first flowers to be the harbinger of spring.

LEFT As winter is a dormant time in the garden, there is less to do outside, and there is more time to spend on being creative with your flower designs. Twigs, cones, old seed heads, and berries are a source of inspiration.

ABOVE Beech hedging holds onto its autumnal leaves, and this makes an interesting pattern when dusted in frost.

ABOVE RIGHT Making letters out of wild hips and holly berries from the Dutch auction has been one of my trademarks in recent years. They are modern, yet reminiscent of Victorian design. I nail them to my garden shed and the boarding on my garden barn for winter decoration.

RIGHT Ivy berries are a winter staple for me. They form the background color of so many of my designs. When the berries fall off in spring I feel bereft for a while, until lots of new summer foliage fills their place.

FAR RIGHT This is the time of year to look for some interesting branches covered in moss. Lichen-covered larch is one of my favorite winter seasonal finds. The moss works well with evergreens, silvers, and gray. I like to use larch in natural designs.

OPPOSITE, CLOCKWISE FROM TOP LEFT Berried ivy is a genus of fifteen or so evergreen ground-creeping or climbing woody plants. The flowers are yellow-green and the fruit is dark purple to black. I adore the texture of *Hedera helix*. Long trails are also useful for Christmas decorations and garlands.

Seed heads are useful in the winter garden as they add interest and look fabulous when dusted with frost, and they also provide feed for the birds. My most prized seed heads are teasels, which attract the highly colored goldfinches with their bright red faces and yellow wing patch.

The spiky leaves of holly have a dusting of "Jack Frost." The overnight frosts of winter accentuate the natural forms of plants and make us appreciate their elegant structures, from their delicate branches down to their leaves and seed heads.

The cypress is a flame-shaped, tapering tree, with but a short stem below its branches, which rise erectly and close to the trunk. The gray varieties, which bear cones, are very useful for decoration.

Blue pine and spruce are invaluable at this time of year. They can be worked into all kinds of decorations and last very well, even when they are not in water. Rarely used at any other time of year, their scent is part of their attraction.

RIGHT Snowdrop bulbs have become highly prized in the winter garden. I buy single and double varieties in their hundreds "in the green" after they have flowered and plant them out in early spring.

what's good to buy

In these days of global transportation there are lots of flowers to buy even in the bleak midwinter. At this time of year I am drawn to more exotic and extravagant flowers, which give great value in centrally heated homes. Members of the orchid family are at their best now, so this is a good time to splurge.

1 *Hippeastrum* 'Tineke Verburg' is a gorgeous deep orange amaryllis that is a new favorite of mine.

2 Anthuriums are extremely long lasting, with some varieties living up to sixty days. This taupe pink variety 'Marijke' is one of around seventy or so available and the shades are much more subtle than the bright red 'Tropical' variety, which is the best known.

3 The orchid x *Cattlianthe* 'Molly Tyler' is a deep pink color with darker magenta trumpets.

4 Cyclamen have long been a popular pot plant in winter, and a Dutch grower has championed the sale of cut cyclamens for vase displays since 2009.

5 Nerine bulbs are jewels in the winter garden. Pink and red varieties are more common than the white *Nerine bowdenii* 'Alba'. The flowers are long lasting, three weeks or more in the garden, or two weeks as a cut flower in water.

6 There are still some gladioli around in the winter. The seasonal red 'Hunting Song' variety is useful in large displays.

7 *Euphorbia fulgens* is a relative of the ubiquitous Christmas poinsettia. This more suave relative has long, arched branches with delicate pointed leaves and dense, dainty white flowers along its elegant curved stems.

8 *Ilex aquifolium*, or English holly, has attractive evergreen dark green glossy leaves and it produces red berries, which make it a decorative plant for the colder months and indispensable for Christmas decorations.

9 Corsican hellebores have prickly edged, gray-green leaves on stout stems holding clusters of large, pale green, upturned flowers with green nectaries and stamens.

10 All cymbidiums are great value, lasting as long as six weeks in water. The mini varieties are often a lot less expensive and are great for cutting down into arrangements. This variety is *Cymbidium* Melinga 'Rum Jungle'.

4

5

7

9

10

8

winter hedge

I asked advice for my winter hedge from William Baird, who runs a family specialist hedge nursery in Dedham Vale on the Suffolk/Essex border in east England. At his nursery, they have over a hundred varieties of hedges and native trees.

I suggested some of the species that I liked to use in my flower arrangements, and he recommended that we have one dominant species. He suggested *Cotoneaster franchetti*, which is invaluable for all-year-round interest. The result would make a good attractive hedge, in which all the species would get on and grow well together. This would be an informal hedge that would give the flower arranger something to snip all the year round, but would be particularly good in winter when the colored stems of the dogwood would look stunning against the winter berries and the foliage. This kind of hedge should be trimmed on each alternate side in late winter to maximize the amount of berry-bearing branches.

1 *Viburnum opulus*
2 *Cornus alba* 'Sibirica'
3 Larch
4 *Corylus avellana* 'Contorta'
5 *Cotoneaster franchetii*
6 *Ilex aquifolium*
7 *Salix babylonica* 'Tortuosa'
8 *Hedera hibernica*
9 Privet varieties
10 *Cornus sanguinea* 'Midwinter Fire'

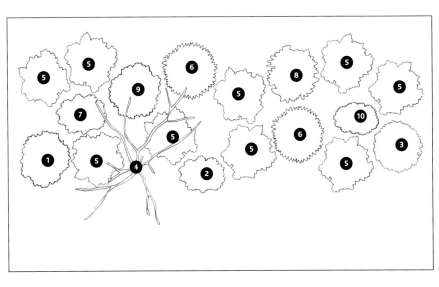

early winter

The melancholy accent of early winter changes the landscape dramatically. Structure and texture dominate my winter walks, and when I get home, scraping the mud off my boots, I contemplate making the house cozier. As each day gets shorter, I turn from the garden to decorate my home.

Flowering plants and displays indoors are essential to get us through the winter gloom. The barren trees and bushes in my garden and the wider landscape and bundles of twigs at the flower market suggest new designs.

I spend more time working with foliages, and I am inevitably drawn more often to fruits and vegetables to inspire my creations. On some mornings the mists seem to meet the garden as everything looks gray. The predominant color in the garden now is the green of the evergreens, my dependable friends at this time of year, and the brown of the mud that buries my favorite herbaceous perennials. My deciduous trees and shrubs take on a new persona as they take their winter break.

Most of the readily available early winter flowers are from the all-year-round stock that the floral industry around the world consistently produces, among them alstromeria, chrysanthemums, carnations, eryngiums, gerberas, lilies, limoniums, molucella, members of the *Ornithogalum* genus (affectionately known as chincherinchee), roses, veronica, and zantedeschia. Seasonal amaranthus, red kangaroo paw, and nerines are still found in the markets. Hybridized lime-green *Viburnum opulus* is also in full flush, although it will not flower in the garden for some months. Forced forsythia is also starting in the early winter.

Myrica gale is an unimposing leafless twig with catkins that is sold in bunches and is useful as a filler for small decorations. It can also be used to edge arrangements or even to weave into garlands and wreaths. It is brown and adds more to structure and texture than to decoration. Tropical leaves are useful, especially dark cordylines and a supply of *Leucothoe fontanesiana* 'Rainbow', which has fabulous markings and is deep red.

LEFT *Cornus sanguinea* is often seen in ancient hedges—most noticeably in September, when it produces plum-colored dark leaves well before most plants have colored up for fall. It has dark fruit on twiggy stems and creates a much more delicate effect than *Cornus alba*.

THIS PAGE The dogwood I
like to use in vases in winter is
Cornus sanguinea 'Midwinter'.
The gradient of color in the
stems from orange, through
yellow to red, is stunning.
Here, it has been used to
simple effect with peach
amaryllis. The glass vase
was lined with pomegranate
slices to hide the base of the
stems and to reflect the
rich-toned colors.

OPPOSITE The cut flower cyclamen has made a comeback and caught the imagination because this delicate bloom, often unreliable as a plant, is actually very long lasting as a cut flower. These pale pink cut cyclamen 'Leonie' are arranged simply in ceramic vases with votives. The new varieties have been bred from fringed, flamed Victoria and Fantasia types. Flowers are harvested in the early morning and an incision made in each stem in order to extend their shelf life.

THIS PAGE I use anthuriums in my own home because they last so well, and I tend to choose them for their color to accent the interior decoration. Here I have used a new variety of very dark anthuriums called 'Black Queen' with a taupe pin variety called 'Marijke'.

totally tropical Most flower lovers like to see a flower in bud, open, evolve, and expire. However, those of us in the trade sometimes need a flower that looks as good on day one as it does seven days later, and the anthurium gets the number one slot in my book for reliability and longevity. They offer great value for money in the winter months. Anthuriums are one of those flowers that you either love or hate. Lots of people don't seem to like flowers that "don't do anything." They arrive and look the same as they do when they die. The main growers of anthuriums have been continually breeding long-lasting varieties so that they can guarantee they last at least thirty days. Some they claim can last forty-eight days and others even longer. Originally from South America, the name is derived from the Greek words "anthos," meaning "flowering," and "oura," meaning "tail." The anthurium selection consists of both pot-grown and cut flower specimens.

singular statements

In recent years it has been the trend to use one variety of flower in an arrangement. Fresh, locally grown chrysanthemums, either under glass or outdoors, offer tremendous value for this treatment. On a practical level these flowers are thirsty so they need to have the water topped up regularly in a vase, and this will be especially important if the flowers are in tubes, like the design here. Usually the flowers can last up to three weeks, depending on their country of origin and how long they have been in transit before they get to you. Chrysanthemums have been cultivated in China for centuries, and in Japan the chrysanthemum is a sacred flower, used in many ceremonies. Explorers and plant hunters brought the flower back from Japan to Europe in the seventeenth century, and since then it has become an immensely important cut flower. The chrysanthemum's name derives from the Greek "chrys" (gold) and "anthemon" (flower), from the flower's original color. This in itself is an astonishing thought, as with the help of time and the keen interest in hybridizing these sturdy flowers, they are now available in every color, even blue, thanks to artificial dying techniques. An amazing flower, it is often maligned and overlooked because it is seen as ordinary and common. Overobliging to humans, it is like a celebrity that has had too much exposure. Enjoy this extraordinary long-lasting flower.

LEFT Spiky *Chrysanthemum* 'Elbrus Pink' is a stunner and has an almost ethereal quality. Here individual heads were used in a striking but simple arrangement. I have given new life to two pruned apple tree branches by giving them a lick of white paint. Each branch was arranged in a tall inexpensive frosted vase, suspended with tubes holding the flowers. Tiny garlands of silver stars were added to give a minimal festive twist.

OPPOSITE Taking one stem of *Cymbidium* 'Rum Jungle' and removing all the heads might seem disrespectful to the natural beauty of the plant, but this act of floral vandalism will result in a stunning array of lots of small arrangements. I wired a few ivy leaves to each head and arranged them in simple clear votives. Old glass French yoghurt pots work well, or tiny glass fishbowls. I placed some unadulturated stems in the larger vase with a few stems of twisted willow.

"These individual flower arrangements are perfect for dotting down a dining table. They can also be used for placement cards or handed out as little party gifts to departing guests."

THIS PAGE For a long rectangular table, I like to use a runner down the center to create an area that can be decorated with vases, storm lanterns, and votives. Here I scattered more cranberries and petals from the carnations along the runner.

celebrating early winter

thanksgiving

Thanksgiving has a mix of European and American Indian origins. Typically in Europe, festivals were held after the harvest to give thanks to God and to feast and party after the hard work of bringing the harvest home. The American Indians also had a similar celebration.

1

2

You will need

- 2 flute-shaped vases
- a selection of seasonal flowers and foliages—I used dianthus, standard carnations, and spiky pink and rounded dark red chrysanthemum flowers
- a bunch of ivy berries
- 5 stems of dark red spray roses
- 5 stems of deep pink roses
- 8 ounces of cranberries
- wire cutters and scissors
- oasis bind wire

1 Create a hand-tied bouquet following the instructions on page 122, securing the stems firmly with bind wire. When using cranberries or other fruits in a vase, it is always better to arrange the fruit without any water first.

2 Trim your hand-tied bunch so that it fits on top of the cranberries. Place fruit around the stems to stabilize the arrangement. Then add the water so that it is full to the top of the vase. At this point I often poke my scissors under the water line to recut the tie, so that it releases the flowers slightly and gives a more natural look.

late winter

Thanksgiving marks the start of the Christmas season and is the biggest shopping weekend in the United States, as the preparations for Christmas get underway. Favorite and reliable flowers in white or red predominate alongside the now starring role of the evergreen foliages.

In the last ten years there has been a huge increase in textural foliages, so ivy, hypericum, and the like are taken off to huge vats to be artificially "enhanced" with spray paints or fake snow. A vegetable that has become a winter staple is the ornamental kale; it also gets dragged off for a lick of paint or a dusting of white powder.

While we use a lot of painted twigs, cones, and seed heads in our work at Christmas, I tend to leave the dyed and dipped flowers for others. The metallics are quite hard to work with; red looks much better with the warmer tones of gold and white suits the grays and silver gilts. My other favorite colors for this time of year are the deeper jewel colors, and purple and pink often work their way into my gold schemes. Orange is currently popular and makes for a lighter feel. White is always the safe option and, like a little black dress, it suits any environment and all tastes.

Favorite flowers at this time of year are the amaryllis, narcissus, and white ornamental cabbages, or kales, nerines,

anemones, tulips, hyacinths, roses, and ranunculus. These look lovely with gray brachyglottis, rosemary, eucalyptus, and spray-painted cones and lotus seed heads.

Great reds at this time of year are amaryllis, gladioli, roses, and the long, berried stems of the leafless holly. Hybridized over years, and sold as a berried stick without leaves on stems reaching 3 feet, these are nature on steroids! Amazing triumphs of man's will over the natural world, not only are they astonishing to look at, these stems last weeks before they drop their berries and become barren twigs.

In the depths of winter I am also drawn to potted succulents as decorations on my outdoor tables. I use them at different heights and sizes in old terra-cotta pots. They often grow in niches or small places; they need very little soil because they have short roots. They also look amazing when spray painted gold and silver for indoor potted table arrangements during the festive season.

The moment Christmas is over it is time to start enjoying the flowers of the new year and the coming season of spring. It is the best time to start to

use pussy willow and the early branches of winter jasmine. The *Betula* genus have great catkins that add movement to arrangements. Twigs and branches are an important component of winter arrangements.

ABOVE LEFT Scented paperwhite narcissus are at their best at this time of year.

ABOVE Roses, both standard and spray, perennially available, are essential for winter decorations.

OPPOSITE An old fruit crate was transformed with rope and moss into a base for a winter arrangement. Cypress supplies the background color with lichen-covered twigs, silver-sprayed lotus seed heads, ornamental kale heads, amaryllis, nerines, and roses all playing their part.

using moss In winter I find myself using moss in far larger quantities than at any other time of the year, both as a base and as part of the design. The Japanese often use moss in their gardens, and old temples sometimes feature moss as a carpet for a forest scene. Moss is thought to add calm and peace to a garden. The use of stones and aggregates also plays a large part of Japanese landscaping, and a similar use of moss and stones in planted displays can also add to the design and the emotion. For the flower arranger there are several important types of moss. The clump-forming bun moss or looser flatter carpet moss are great for covering bulbs or mechanics in arrangements. Sometimes we use decorative green bun moss as part of the design, as its deep green velvety texture adds depth to arrangements. Spanish moss and reindeer moss are also used in planted arrangements, and sphagnum moss is essential for the base of Christmas wreaths. Most mosses can survive desiccation, sometimes for months and even seasons. Most return to life within a few hours of wet weather. Carpet moss forms on trees and branches in a shady area in the winter and after a wet spell can make a walk in the forest quite magical.

LEFT With its soft gray buds, pussy willow is the teddy bear of the season, cuddly and tactile. Here, on a soft bed of moss, green and white hellebores emerge as if they are growing through a vertical and horizontal grid of pussy willow.

OPPOSITE In this huge glass tank I lined narcissus bulbs with sphagnum moss set on distinct layers of vine, stones, and stripes of aggregate. This is the best time to use bulbs indoors, making them into windowsill arrangements with stones and mosses.

branches and twigs These can give structure, height, and grace, or they can be used to create the mechanics or structure for the flowers. Use the habitat of the tree to your advantage. Branches that naturally grow upright add height, while arched branches give downward movement to a design. Groups of twigs, such as dogwood, birch, and cinnamon, are a useful and inexpensive device to add interest in your winter floral designs. Of course, you can add a lick of spray paint for color. Even the disused lower part of a flower can work, such as woody stemmed roses or knobbly carnation stems. Waste products get recycled more at this time of year, when flowers and foliage are in short supply.

LEFT Groupings of foliages and cut stems tied together with a few flowers are an inexpensive way of creating a table center. Spikes of green dogwood and cinnamon sticks have also been spiraled into the design to add interest and texture. Small apples can be wired onto kebob sticks or bamboo garden canes to add inexpensive and long-lasting color.

OPPOSITE A simple vase of long-lasting amaryllis flowers is given a more dynamic form with the addition of spiky twigs. I chose these branches because they look aged and interesting. They are from an alder tree found in the hedge that separates my garden from that of my neighbors. I also adore old fruit trees for this kind of look as they have very curved branches.

"The bare branches of winter and the lack of seasonal flower can in itself be an inspiration. Once the leaves have gone we can appreciate the lichen on the bare branches and use the structure in designs."

christmas

There is nothing like a fresh Christmas tree in your home for the festive season—the scent of a real fir or spruce tree is delicious. Trees are sold either cut or potted. Very often even if they are in a pot, they will have been recently dug up and placed in a pot for sale for the festive season.

Whichever you decide to have, the most important thing is to remember to keep the tree watered. If you choose a large tree it will inevitably have been cut and it is just like a flower. It needs water to survive, and I prefer the reservoir-style tree holders in which you can let your tree stand in a few inches of water. The trees are usually very thirsty when you first bring them indoors and it is not at all a bad idea to recut the bottom of the stem when you get the tree back home and let it condition in a bucket with some flower food for a few hours before bringing indoors. When inside, keep the reservoir topped up daily, and you can even buy some special tree food for Christmas trees to prolong their life.

LEFT Christmas is an important time for scent. I adore the smell of a fresh fir tree recently placed indoors. Add some citrus and cinnamon and it is pretty perfect!

ABOVE Peanuts with a touch of gold spray paint make organic garlands when wired together with reel wire.

OPPOSITE Natural, simple decorations in the Scandinavian style was the theme for this tree. I tend to alternate between over-the-top exuberance and simplicity each year. However the tree ends up, I always use birch twigs horizontally on the branches so that the tree has more structure and texture.

RIGHT A clementines was suspended with raffia to give scent and color.

BELOW Collect cones when on woodland walk and save them for the winter. Spruce them up with spray paint and wire them to the tree branches. If you store them in your attic you can change the color the next year; they are the perfect recyclable and adaptable decoration.

BELOW RIGHT Groups of cinnamon sticks were wired together with a decorative colored bead wire to hang on the tree.

dressing the tree When you decorate a tree there are certain things to remember. After the water, you will need around one hundred lights per foot of your tree for a well-lit tree. I often like to add sprayed birch twigs to give the tree a better shape. Some years I use one color for a more sophisticated look, and then the next year I alternate with a really multicolored theme, so I can bring out all my old favorite decorations from over the years. I also try to incorporate some scent with cinnamon, cloves, and star anise. You need lots of different shapes and textures when decorating to get a good look.

"This charming arrangement does not require any complicated techniques, and the damage to the evergreens in your garden is minimal."

THIS PAGE Simple glass bottles arranged in a circle make an easy and affordable Christmas ring. Here, I used a little green food dye and a few sprigs of foliage and berries from my garden. This works well in any season with a few flowers and a little color in the water.

advent rings Advent rings in the window of a flower shop in London were one of the things that attracted me to a career in floristry, so I always have a soft spot for them. This frame was snapped up in Ikea on one of those shopping trips to the famous store where you go in for one thing and end up with a truck load! You can also make your own rings out of shaped wire coat hangers or ask a fabricator or blacksmith (sourced online) to make you a custom-made frame that you can use for years to come. The two wreaths on these pages show how you can use them on flat surfaces or suspended on ribbons, as well as in the traditional way hung flat on a door or wall.

THIS PAGE Red plump chili peppers were threaded on a wire and wound through a touch of muehlenbeckia vine, some ivy trails, and some dried red apples. Velvet bows, gold pearls, and red candles add a more traditional touch.

working with evergreens

a festive swag

This is far easier to make than a door wreath and just as effective. You need some flat foliage, such as a stem of pine, yew, or cypress, and then a good assortment of evergreens to give texture and color as well as shape. Eucalyptus or rosemary works well if you want gray tones, and it also gives scent.

You will need

- some flat foliage such as spruce, yew, or cypress
- some variegated foliage—I used variegated holly
- some trailing foliage, such as ivy
- some berried foliage, such as ivy, cotoneaster, or holly
- bind wire
- floristry scissors
- sewing scissors
- 6 feet wire-edged ribbon, at least 1½ inches wide

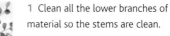

1 Clean all the lower branches of material so the stems are clean.

2 Take a stem of flat foliage as your base, and then add another stem to the left and right of it.

3 Now start to build your swag. You are aiming for a diamond shape in outline, but a triangular one in profile. Build up the center

by adding the busy stems. Add berries and variegated foliage to all sides. The back should still be flat, but the stems should now be spiraled so that the profile is pronounced and not flat.

4 Tie very tightly with bind wire, which is a paper-covered wire that is used in the industry to make tied bunches.

5 Next you need to make your bow. This is much easier if you have one-sided ribbon that is wire edged. Make two loops holding the center of the loop.

6 Continue until you have made three loops. Cut off the end of the ribbon (leaving about 20 inches). Usually floristry scissors do not cut ribbon so you need to have a sewing pair. Finally, add the bow to the bottom of your swag and then wire it onto the door.

index

5 Next you need to make your bow. This is much easier if you have one-sided ribbon that is wire edged. Make two loops holding the center of the loop.

6 Continue until you have made three loops. Cut off the end of the ribbon (leaving about 20 inches). Usually floristry scissors do not cut ribbon so you need to have a sewing pair. Finally, add the bow to the bottom of your swag and then wire it onto the door.

index

acknowledgments

It has been an absolute pleasure to work on this very personal book at my home in the country with a wonderful, talented, handpicked team, selected as always by my accomplished publisher and dear friend Jacqui Small. Thank you to all the team at head office in London, especially Kerenza Swift and Liz Somers. Thanks also to Peter Colley for his role in producing the book. Enormous appreciation and gratitude are due to my wonderful editor Sian Parkhouse, who has been encouraging and patient in all the right doses! I was delighted and honored to be able to work with such a talented photographer and I adore Rachel Whiting's gorgeous photos of my flowers and arrangements. Thank you also to Corin Ashleigh Brown for all her hard work in assisting Rachel and all of us at the shoots. My grateful thanks also go to Sarah Rock, who designed this beautiful book. Her creative eye has been vital to the overall look of this project.

This book would not have existed without the help of many of the horticulturalists who have inspired and helped me in my own garden:

William Baird from Glebe Farm Hedging for the wonderful tapestry hedge design (pp. 134–35) and all his helpful suggestions on how to keep us busy arranging berries and foliage in the winter months. www.hedge-plants.co.uk

Roger Harvey for this help and advice in my own garden and for letting me pick from his nusery. Also for the uplifting spring border design (pp. 24–25). www.harveysgardenplants.co.uk

Michael Loftus for his insights on plants and to Viv Kemp for the beautiful summer border design (pp. 64–65). www.woottensplants.co.uk

Jekka McVicar for her advice and stunning design for our herb garden border (pp. 98–99). www.jekkasherbfarm.com.

On a horticultural note I would also like to thank Tony Lord, our botanical expert.

It was lovely to have the opportunity to work with hugely talented Hannah McVicar, who so beautifully illustrated our four seasonal borders.

Thanks to my wonderful and loyal staff in London and those who have helped out at home, too. Special thanks are due to Anita Everard for sharing her talents and being so inspirational on this book. A big thank-you to Hisako Watanabe who worked on location and Anne Cadle and Tania Newman for their support back at base. Thanks also to Penny Pizzey, Ann Pochetty, and Gina Jay for their support and friendship.

Heartfelt thanks to Damian Michalak for helping to fulfill my dream of always having something to pick in the garden. Thanks also to Nigel Clark and all at Lawnorder. Locally, too, I would like to thank Lynne Noble for looking after the team and for letting us photograph her 'Charlotte' rose (p. 55) and also Garrads Boutique Hotel. Finally thanks to Raymundo, Connie, and Cosmos who chase all the hungry bunnies away!

www.paula-pryke-flowers.com

All photography is by Rachel Whiting except for the following pages, which are by Tara Fisher:
6, 7, 8 bottom left, 9 bottom right, 10, 11, 57 center top, 57 bottom left, 58 center top, 58 bottom right, 59, 62, 91 top, 93 top row, 93 bottom right, 100 bottom left, 106,107, 108, 109, 110, 111, 148,149